COMMON CORE

LANGUAGE ARTS & LITERACY

Activities that Captivate, Motivate, & Reinforce

REVISED EDITION

Grade 5

by Marjorie Frank

IncentivePublications

BY WORLD BOOK

a Scott Fetzer company

Illustrated by Kathleen Bullock
Cover by Penny Laporte

Print Edition ISBN 978-0-86530-744-5
E-book Edition ISBN 978-1-62950-199-4 (PDF)

World Book, Inc.
233 North Michigan Avenue
Suite 2000
Chicago, Illinois, 60601 U.S.A.

For information about World Book and Incentive Publications products, call **1-800-967-5325,** or visit our websites at **www.worldbook.com** and **www.incentivepublications.com.**

Printed in the United States of America by Sheridan Books, Inc.
Chelsea, Michigan
1st Printing June 2014

CONTENTS

Introduction

Great Support for Common Core State Standards! 7

How to Use This Book 7

About Common Core State Standards for Language Arts & Literacy 8

Grade 5 Common Core State Standards for Language Arts & Literacy

College and Career Readiness Anchor Standards for Reading, Grades K–12 9

Reading Standards for Literature, Grade 5 10

Reading Standards for Informational Text, Grade 5 11

Reading Standards: Foundational Skills for Grade 5 12

College and Career Readiness Anchor Standards for Writing, Grades K–12 13

Writing Standards, Grade 5 14

College and Career Readiness Anchor Standards
    for Speaking and Listening, Grades K–12 16

Speaking and Listening Standards, Grade 5 17

College and Career Readiness Anchor Standards for Language, Grades K–12 . . . 18

Language Standards, Grade 5 19

Reading—Literature

Adventures Unlimited *(word meaning, context)* 22

Explore a Deep Cave *(word meaning, context)* 24

Test-Drive a Cool Car *(word meaning, context)* 25

Meet a Great Artist *(evidence from text)* 26

Dine with the Forty-Niners *(evidence from text)* 27

Rock into the Past *(evidence from text)* 28

Ride the High Seas *(evidence from text)* 29

Join the Circus! *(theme, summarize)* 30

Ride the *Orient Express (theme, summarize)* 31

Follow Clues with Sherlock *(summarize)* 32

Navigate a Raging River *(theme, summarize)* 33

Visit a Grand Palace *(character, setting, events)* 34

Be a Judge for the Day *(character, setting, events)* 36

Catch a Leprechaun *(structure of text)* 37

See Your Name in Lights *(point of view)* 38

Catch a Big Wave *(visual elements)* 40

Prepare to Say "Wow!" *(visual elements)* 41

Take a Daring Ride *(compare, contrast texts)* 42

Read Some New Old News *(compare, contrast texts)* 44

Reading—Informational Text

Join a Sleuth Academy *(evidence from text)* 46

Check Out Some Curious Cases *(evidence from text)* 47

Learn to Make a Mummy *(evidence from text)* 48

Race with the Dogs *(evidence from text)* 49

Explore the Sunken *Titanic* *(key ideas, details, summarize)* 50

Specialize in Surveillance *(key ideas, details, summarize)* 51

Hang Out with Paul Bunyan *(key ideas, details, summarize)* 52

Explore Mysterious Atlantis *(key ideas, details, summarize)* 53

Snoop Around the Ocean *(academic vocabulary)* 54

Eavesdrop on History *(academic vocabulary)* 55

Head to the Space Station *(text structure)* 56

Crack the Cases! *(compare accounts)* 58

Take a Ride with "The King" *(text structure)* 60

Follow a Crime-Line *(draw information from source)* .61

Be a Human Spider *(draw information from source)* .62

Drop into the Alps *(draw information from source)* 63

Cheer for the Slugs *(reasons, evidence)* 64

Visit Camelot *(reasons, evidence)* 66

Search for Nessie *(integrate information)* 67

Reading—Foundational Skills

Beach Misbehavior *(phonics, word recognition, affixes)* 70

Danger at Sea *(phonics, word recognition, affixes)* 71

Unforgettable! *(word recognition, affixes, roots)* 72

Below the Sea *(word recognition, affixes, roots)* 73

An Unusual Discovery *(phonics, word recognition, compounds)* 74

A Brake in the Peer *(phonics, word recognition, homophones)* 75

What You See in the Sea *(phonics, word recognition, homophones)* 76

Where Would You Find This? *(word recognition, unfamiliar words)* 77

Where Would You Find That? *(word recognition, unfamiliar words)* 78

Writing

In My Opinion *(text types: opinion)* 80

Convince Me! *(text types: opinion)* 82

Terrible Choices *(text types: informative/explanatory)* 83

Great Food—Your Way *(text types: informative/explanatory)* 84

Rock in the Future *(text types: narrative)* 85

Cliffhangers *(text types: narrative)* 86

Words on the Move *(produce writing)* 88

Weathered Words *(produce writing)* 89

Ask Me Anything! *(produce writing)* 90

What Characters! *(produce writing)* 92

Picture This *(produce writing)* 94

Straight From the Pages *(evidence from literature)* 95

Evidence, Please! *(evidence from informational text)* 96

Language

Marooned and Terrorized and . . . *(conventions: conjunctions)* 98

Bon Voyage! *(conventions: prepositions)* 99

Yikes! (conventions: interjections) 100

After Dark (conventions: verb tenses) 101

What's Happening? (conventions: verb tenses) 102

A Shifting Story (conventions: verb tenses) 103

Watch Out, Crab! (conventions: comma use) 104

Along the Boardwalk (conventions: comma use) 105

Beach Reading (conventions: punctuating titles) 106

Misfits in the Sand (conventions: spelling) 107

Trouble in the Surf (conventions: spelling) 108

Beach-Blanket Errors (conventions: spelling) 109

Swimmers' Line-Up (language use) 110

Shop Talk (language use) 111

Beach Conversations (language use) 112

Hot Beach, Cool Drinks (vocabulary: context) 113

Sunken Treasure (vocabulary: context) 114

How Many Whales? (vocabulary: context) 115

A Biped on a Unicycle (vocabulary: affixes, roots) 116

Shark Alert (vocabulary: affixes, roots) 117

Could You? Would You? Should You? (vocabulary: consult references) 118

What Would You Do with It? (vocabulary: consult references) 119

Ho Hum (vocabulary: figurative language) 120

Happy as a Clam (vocabulary: figurative language) 121

Good Taste in Friends (vocabulary: figurative language) 122

The Beach Connection (vocabulary: word relationships) 123

Don't Obey the Signs (vocabulary: word relationships) 124

A Whale or a Wail? (vocabulary: word relationships) 125

Making Waves (academic vocabulary) 126

Assessment and Answer Keys

Language Arts & Literacy Assessment 128

Assessment Answer Key 139

Activities Answer Key 140

Great Support for Common Core State Standards!

Invite your students to join in on mysteries and adventures with colorful characters! They will delight in the high-appeal topics and engaging visuals. They can

. . . fend off sharks at the shore and pirates on a deserted island,

. . . decide whether or not to take a barrel ride over Niagara Falls,

. . . watch an altercation between a giant squid and a fierce octopus,

. . . explain the mystery of a sunken treasure chest,

. . . study at a super-sleuth academy and crack curious cases,

. . . take a ride on a stomach-flipping roller coaster,

. . . soar on a rocket to the International Space Station,

. . . drop in on a Stone Age rock-and-roll concert,

. . . join the search for the Loch Ness Monster,

. . . and tackle many other engaging ventures.

And while they join in these adventures, they will be moving toward competence in critical language skills and standards that they need for success in the real world.

How to Use This Book

- The pages are tools to support your teaching of the concepts, processes, and skills outlined in the Common Core State Standards. This is not a curriculum; it is a collection of engaging experiences for you to use as you work with your students or children.

- Use any given page to introduce, explain, teach, practice, extend, assess, start a discussion about, or get students collaborating on a skill or concept.

- Use any page in a large-group or small-group setting to deepen understandings and expand knowledge or skills. **Pages are not meant to be used as independent work. Guide students in their use. Do them together. Review and discuss the work with students.**

- Each activity is focused on a particular standard or cluster of standards, but most make use of or can be expanded to strengthen other standards as well.

- The book is organized according to the Common Core language strands. Use the tables on pages 9 to 20, the page labels, and notations on the Contents pages to identify the standards supported by each page.

- Use the suggestions on page 8 for further mastery of the Common Core State Standards for Language Arts & Literacy.

About Common Core State Standards for Language Arts & Literacy

The Common Core State Standards for Language Arts & Literacy at Grade 5 aim to build strong content knowledge across a wide range of subject areas. They are also designed to develop capabilities for thoughtful use of technology and digital media; for finding, applying, and evaluating evidence; for working and thinking independently; and for deepening reasoning and understanding. To best help students gain and master these robust standards for reading, writing, speaking, listening, and language:

1. Know the standards well. Keep them in front of you. Understand for yourself the big picture of what the standards seek to do. (See www.corestandards.org.)

2. Work to apply, expand, and deepen student skills. With activities in this book (or any learning activities), plan to include

    . . . interaction with peers—in pairs, small groups, and large groups.

    . . . plenty of discussion and integration of language content.

    . . . emphasis on asking questions, analyzing, careful reading and listening, finding evidence, and reasoning.

    . . . lots of observation, meaningful feedback, follow-up, and reflection.

3. Ask questions that advance reasoning, discernment, relevance, and real-life connection:

   - *Why? What does this mean?*
   - *How do you know?*
   - *What led you to this conclusion?*
   - *Where did you find this?*
   - *What else do you know (or need to know)?*
   - *What is the evidence?*
   - *Where else could you look?*
   - *How is _____ like (or unlike) _____?*
   - *What would be another viewpoint?*
   - *Why do you think that?*
   - *What is the purpose?*
   - *What belief does the author have?*
   - *Do you agree? Why or why not?*
   - *How does this part affect that part?*
   - *Where have you seen something like this before?*
   - *How are the words used?*
   - *What are the parts? How do they work together?*
   - *How does the text confirm your ideas?*
   - *How would this vary for a different purpose, place, person, or situation?*
   - *How does the idea of the text (or speech or argument) build?*
   - *How is this idea affected by the ideas that came before it?*
   - *How could you write (or say) this to give _____ effect?*
   - *What is the effect of using this word (or phrase, or idea, or structure)?*
   - *How is this affected by the writer's (or speaker's) perspective or culture?*
   - *So what? (What difference does this information, or perspective, or discovery make?)*

Grade 5 Common Core State Standards
for Language Arts & Literacy

College and Career Readiness Anchor Standards (CCRS) for Reading, Grades K–12

Standard Number	Standard	Pages that Support
Key Ideas and Details		
CCRA.R.1	Read closely to determine what the text says explicitly and to make logical inferences from it; cite specific textual evidence when writing or speaking to support conclusions drawn from the text.	22-23, 24, 25, 26, 27, 28, 29, 30, 31, 32, 33, 34-35, 36, 37, 38-39, 40, 41, 42-43, 44, 46, 47, 48, 49, 50, 51, 52, 53, 54, 55, 56-57, 58-59, 60, 61, 62, 63, 64-65, 66, 67, 68
CCRA.R.2	Determine central ideas or themes of a text and analyze their development; summarize the key supporting details and ideas.	30, 31, 32, 33, 46, 47, 48, 49, 50, 51, 52, 53, 60
CCRA.R.3	Analyze how and why individuals, events, and ideas develop and interact over the course of a text.	34-35, 36, 46, 48, 50, 53, 56-57, 62, 63, 64-65, 67, 68
Craft and Structure		
CCRA.R.4	Interpret words and phrases as they are used in a text, including determining technical, connotative, and figurative meanings, and analyze how specific word choices shape meaning or tone.	22-23, 24, 25, 54, 55
CCRA.R.5	Analyze the structure of texts, including how specific sentences, paragraphs, and larger portions of the text (e.g., a section, chapter, scene, or stanza) relate to each other and the whole.	37, 42-43, 56-57, 58-59
CCRA.R.6	Assess how point of view or purpose shapes the content and style of a text.	38-39, 56-57, 58-59
Integration of Knowledge and Ideas		
CCRA.R.7	Integrate and evaluate content presented in diverse media and formats, including visually and quantitatively, as well as in words.	40, 41, 46, 47, 48, 49, 50, 51, 52, 53, 56-57, 58-59, 61, 62, 63, 64-65, 66, 67, 68
CCRA.R.8	Delineate and evaluate the argument and specific claims in a text, including the validity of the reasoning as well as the relevance and sufficiency of the evidence.	38-39, 40, 41, 64-65, 66, 67
CCRA.R.9	Analyze how two or more texts address similar themes or topics in order to build knowledge or to compare the approaches the authors take.	42-43, 44, 67, 68
Range of Reading and Level of Text Complexity		
CCRA.R.10	Read and comprehend complex literary and informational texts independently and proficiently.	22–45, 46–68

Copyright © 2014 World Book, Inc./
Incentive Publications, Chicago, IL

Common Core Reinforcement Activities: 5th Grade Language

Reading Standards for Literature, Grade 5

Standard Number	Standard	Pages that Support
Key Ideas and Details		
RL.5.1	Quote accurately from a text when explaining what the text says explicitly and when drawing inferences from the text.	22-23, 24, 25, 26, 27, 28, 29, 30, 31, 32, 33, 34-35, 36, 37, 38-39, 40, 41, 42-43, 44
RL.5.2	Determine a theme of a story, drama, or poem from details in the text, including how characters in a story or drama respond to challenges or how the speaker in a poem reflects upon a topic; summarize the text.	30, 31, 32, 33
RL.5.3	Compare and contrast two or more characters, settings, or events in a story or drama, drawing on specific details in the text (e.g., how characters interact).	34-35, 36
Craft and Structure		
RL.5.4	Determine the meaning of words and phrases as they are used in a text, including figurative language such as metaphors and similes.	22-23, 24, 25
RL.5.5	Explain how a series of chapters, scenes, or stanzas fits together to provide the overall structure of a particular story, drama, or poem.	37, 42-43, 44
RL.5.6	Describe how a narrator's or speaker's point of view influences how events are described.	38-39
Integration of Knowledge and Ideas		
RL.5.7	Analyze how visual and multimedia elements contribute to the meaning, tone, or beauty of a text (e.g., graphic novel, multimedia presentation of fiction, folktale, myth, poem).	40, 41
RL.5.8	(Not applicable to literature.)	*Not covered.*
RL.5.9	Compare and contrast stories in the same genre (e.g., mysteries and adventure stories) on their approaches to similar themes and topics.	42-43, 44
Range of Reading and Level of Text Complexity		
RL.5.10	By the end of the year, read and comprehend literature, including stories, dramas, and poetry, at the high end of the grades 4–5 text complexity band independently and proficiently.	22-44

Reading Standards for Informational Text, Grade 5

Standard Number	Standard	Pages that Support
Key Ideas and Details		
RI.5.1	Quote accurately from a text when explaining what the text says explicitly and when drawing inferences from the text.	46, 47, 48, 49, 50, 51, 52, 53, 54, 55, 56-57, 58-59, 60, 61, 62, 63, 64-65, 66, 67, 68
RI.5.2	Determine two or more main ideas of a text and explain how they are supported by key details; summarize the text.	46, 47, 48, 49, 50, 51, 52, 53, 60
RI.5.3	Explain the relationships or interactions between two or more individuals, events, ideas, or concepts in a historical, scientific, or technical text based on specific information in the text.	46, 48, 50, 53, 56-57, 62, 63, 64-65, 67, 68
Craft and Structure		
RI.5.4	Determine the meaning of general academic and domain-specific words or phrases in a text relevant to a grade 5 topic or subject area.	54, 55
RI.5.5	Compare and contrast the overall structure (e.g., chronology, comparison, cause/effect, problem/solution) of events, ideas, concepts, or information in two or more texts.	56-57, 58-59
RI.5.6	Analyze multiple accounts of the same event or topic, noting important similarities and differences in the point of view they represent.	56-57, 58-59
Integration of Knowledge and Ideas		
RI.5.7	Draw on information from multiple print or digital sources, demonstrating the ability to locate an answer to a question quickly or to solve a problem efficiently.	46, 47, 48, 49, 50, 51, 52, 53, 56-57, 58-59, 61, 62, 63, 64-65, 66, 67, 68
RI.5.8	Explain how an author uses reasons and evidence to support particular points in a text, identifying which reasons and evidence support which point(s).	64-65, 66, 67
RI.5.9	Integrate information from several texts on the same topic in order to write or speak about the subject knowledgeably.	67, 68
Range of Reading and Level of Text Complexity		
RI.5.10	By the end of year, read and comprehend informational texts, including history/social studies, science, and technical texts, at the high end of the grades 4–5 text complexity band independently and proficiently.	46-68

Reading Standards: Foundational Skills for Grade 5

Standard Number	Standard	Pages that Support
Phonics and Word Recognition		
RF.K-1.1	(Kindergarten and Grade 1 Standard)	*Not covered.*
RF.K-1.2	(Kindergarten and Grade 1 Standard)	*Not covered.*
RF.5.3	Know and apply grade-level phonics and word analysis skills in decoding words.	70-78
RF.5.3a	Use combined knowledge of all letter-sound correspondences, syllabication patterns, and morphology (e.g., roots and affixes) to read accurately unfamiliar multisyllabic words in context and out of context.	70, 71, 72, 73, 74, 75, 76, 77, 78
Fluency		
RF.5.4	Read with sufficient accuracy and fluency to support comprehension.	*See note below.*
RF.5.4a	Read on-level text with purpose and understanding.	*See note below.*
RF.5.4b	Read on-level prose and poetry orally with accuracy, appropriate rate, and expression on successive readings.	*See note below.*
RF.5.4c	Use context to confirm or self-correct word recognition and understanding, rereading as necessary.	*See note below.*

Standard 4: *To nourish and assess fluency, it is necessary to listen to students read aloud and/or discuss with them the texts they read. Many pages in this book include stories, questions, or other texts that can be used to support or develop fluency and its connection to comprehension.*

College and Career Readiness Anchor Standards (CCRS) for Writing, Grades K-12

Standard Number	Standard	Pages that Support
Text Types and Purposes		
CCRA.W.1	Write arguments to support claims in an analysis of substantive topics or texts, using valid reasoning and relevant and sufficient evidence.	80-81, 82
CCRA.W.2	Write informative/explanatory texts to examine and convey complex ideas and information clearly and accurately through the effective selection, organization, and analysis of content.	83, 84
CCRA.W.3	Write narratives to develop real or imagined experiences or events using effective technique, well-chosen details, and well-structured event sequences.	85, 86-87
Production and Distribution of Writing		
CCRA.W.4	Produce clear and coherent writing in which the development, organization, and style are appropriate to task, purpose, and audience.	80-81, 82, 83, 84, 85, 86-87, 88, 89, 90-91, 92-93, 94, 95, 96
CCRA.W.5	Develop and strengthen writing as needed by planning, revising, editing, rewriting, or trying a new approach.	80-81, 82, 83, 84, 85, 86-87, 88, 89, 90-91, 92-93, 94, 95, 96
CCRA.W.6	Use technology, including the Internet, to produce and publish writing and to interact and collaborate with others.	*See note below.*
Research to Build and Present Knowledge		
CCRA.W.7	Conduct short as well as more sustained research projects based on focused questions, demonstrating understanding of the subject under investigation.	90-91
CCRA.W.8	Gather relevant information from multiple print and digital sources, assess the credibility and accuracy of each source, and integrate the information while avoiding plagiarism.	95, 96
CCRA.W.9	Draw evidence from literary or informational texts to support analysis, reflection, and research.	95, 96
Range of Writing		
CCRA.W.10	Write routinely over extended time frames (time for research, reflection, and revision) and shorter time frames (a single sitting or a day or two) for a range of tasks, purposes, and audiences.	80-96

Standard 6: *Use technology as a part of your approach for any of the activities in this writing section. Students can create, dictate, photograph, scan, enhance with art or color, or share any of the products they create as a part of these pages.*

Writing Standards for Grade 5

Standard Number	Standard	Pages that Support
Text Types and Purposes		
W.5.1	Write opinion pieces on topics or texts, supporting a point of view with reasons and information.	80-81, 82
W.5.1a	Introduce a topic or text clearly, state an opinion, and create an organizational structure in which related ideas are grouped to support the writer's purpose.	80-81, 82
W.5.1b	Provide logically ordered reasons that are supported by facts and details.	80-81, 82
W.5.1c	Link opinion and reasons using words, phrases, and clauses (e.g., *consequently, specifically*).	80-81, 82
W.5.1d	Provide a concluding statement or section related to the opinion presented.	80-81, 82
W.5.2	Write informative/explanatory texts to examine a topic and convey ideas and information clearly.	83-84
W.5.2a	Introduce a topic clearly, provide a general observation and focus, and group related information logically; include formatting (e.g., headings), illustrations, and multimedia when useful to aiding comprehension.	83, 84
W.5.2b	Develop the topic with facts, definitions, concrete details, quotations, or other information and examples related to the topic.	83, 84
W.5.2c	Link ideas within and across categories of information using words, phrases, and clauses (e.g., *in contrast, especially*).	83, 84
W.5.2d	Use precise language and domain-specific vocabulary to inform about or explain the topic.	83, 84
W.5.2e	Provide a concluding statement or section related to the information or explanation presented.	83, 84
W.5.3	Write narratives to develop real or imagined experiences or events using effective technique, descriptive details, and clear event sequences.	85-87
W.5.3a	Orient the reader by establishing a situation and introducing a narrator and/or characters; organize an event sequence that unfolds naturally.	85, 86-87
W.5.3b	Use narrative techniques, such as dialogue, description, and pacing, to develop experiences and events or show the responses of characters to situations.	85, 86-87
W.5.3c	Use a variety of transitional words, phrases, and clauses to manage the sequence of events.	85, 86-87
W.5.3d	Use concrete words and phrases and sensory details to convey experiences and events precisely.	85, 86-87
W.5.3e	Provide a conclusion that follows from the narrated experiences or events.	85, 86-87

Writing standards continue on next page.

Writing Standards for Grade 5, continued

Standard Number	Standard	Pages that Support
Production and Distribution of Writing		
W.5.4	Produce clear and coherent writing in which the development and organization are appropriate to task, purpose, and audience. (Grade-specific expectations for writing types are defined in writing standards 1–3.)	80-81, 82, 83, 84, 85, 86-87, 88, 89, 90-91, 92-93, 94, 95, 96
W.5.5	With guidance and support from peers and adults, develop and strengthen writing as needed by planning, revising, editing, rewriting, or trying a new approach.	80-81, 82, 83, 84, 85, 86-87, 88, 89, 90-91, 92-93, 94, 95, 96
W.5.6	With some guidance and support from adults, use technology, including the Internet, to produce and publish writing as well as to interact and collaborate with others; demonstrate sufficient command of keyboarding skills to type a minimum of two pages in a single sitting.	*See note below.*
Research to Build and Present Knowledge		
W.5.7	Conduct short research projects that build knowledge through investigation of different aspects of a topic.	90-91
W.5.8	Recall relevant information from experiences or gather relevant information from print and digital sources; summarize or paraphrase information in notes and finished work, and provide a list of sources.	95, 96
W.5.9	Draw evidence from literary or informational texts to support analysis, reflection, and research.	95-96
W.5.9a	Apply grade 5 Reading standards to literature (e.g., "Compare and contrast two or more characters, settings, or events in a story or a drama, drawing on specific details in the text (e.g., how characters interact)").	95
W.5.9b	Apply grade 5 Reading standards to informational texts (e.g., "Explain how an author uses reasons and evidence to support particular points in a text, identifying which reasons and evidence support which point(s)").	96
Range of Writing		
W.5.10	Write routinely over extended time frames (time for research, reflection, and revision) and shorter time frames (a single sitting or a day or two) for a range of discipline-specific tasks, purposes, and audiences.	80-96

Standard 6: *Use technology as a part of your approach for any of the activities in this writing section. Students can create, dictate, photograph, scan, enhance with art or color, or share any of the products they create as a part of these pages.*

College and Career Readiness Anchor Standards (CCRS) for Speaking and Listening, Grades K–12

Standard Number	Standard
Comprehension and Collaboration	
CCRA.SL.1	Prepare for and participate effectively in a range of conversations and collaborations with diverse partners, building on others' ideas and expressing their own clearly and persuasively.
CCRA.SL.2	Integrate and evaluate information presented in diverse media and formats, including visually, quantitatively, and orally.
CCRA.SL.3	Evaluate a speaker's point of view, reasoning, and use of evidence and rhetoric.
Presentation of Knowledge and Ideas	
CCRA.SL.4	Present information, findings, and supporting evidence such that listeners can follow the line of reasoning and the organization, development, and style are appropriate to task, purpose, and audience.
CCRA.SL.5	Make strategic use of digital media and visual displays of data to express information and enhance understanding of presentations.
CCRA.SL.6	Adapt speech to a variety of contexts and communicative tasks, demonstrating command of formal English when indicated or appropriate.

Speaking and Listening Standards: *The speaking and listening standards are not specifically addressed in this book. However, most pages can be used for conversation and collaboration. Teachers and parents are encouraged to use the activities in a sharing and discussion format. Many of the pages include visual information that students can include in the integration and evaluation of information.*

In addition, most of the texts and activities can be adapted to listening activities or can be used to support the listening and speaking standards.

Speaking and Listening Standards for Grade 5

Standard Number	Standard
Comprehension and Collaboration	
SL.5.1	Engage effectively in a range of collaborative discussions (one-on-one, in groups, and teacher-led) with diverse partners on grade 5 topics and texts, building on others' ideas and expressing their own clearly.
SL.5.1a	Come to discussions prepared, having read or studied required material; explicitly draw on that preparation and other information known about the topic to explore ideas under discussion.
SL.5.1b	Follow agreed-upon rules for discussions and carry out assigned roles.
SL.5.1c	Pose and respond to specific questions to clarify or follow up on information, and make comments that contribute to the discussion and link to the remarks of others.
SL.5.1d	Review the key ideas expressed and explain their own ideas and understanding in light of the discussion.
SL.5.2	Summarize a written text read aloud or information presented in diverse media and formats, including visually, quantitatively, and orally.
SL.5.3	Summarize the points a speaker makes and explain how each claim is supported by reasons and evidence.
Presentation of Knowledge and Ideas	
SL.5.4	Report on a topic or text or present an opinion, sequencing ideas logically and using appropriate facts and relevant, descriptive details to support main ideas or themes; speak clearly at an understandable pace.
SL.5.5	Include multimedia components (e.g., graphics, sound) and visual displays in presentations when appropriate to enhance the development of main ideas or themes.
SL.5.6	Adapt speech to a variety of contexts and tasks, using formal English when appropriate to task and situation.

Speaking and Listening Standards: *The speaking and listening standards are not specifically addressed in this book. However, most pages can be used for conversation and collaboration. Teachers and parents are encouraged to use the activities in a sharing and discussion format. Many of the pages include visual information that students can include in the integration and evaluation of information.*

In addition, most of the texts and activities can be adapted to listening activities or can be used to support the listening and speaking standards.

College and Career Readiness Anchor Standards (CCRS) for Language, Grades K-12

Standard Number	Standard	Pages that Support
Conventions of Standard English		
CCRA.L.1	Demonstrate command of the conventions of standard English grammar and usage when writing or speaking.	98, 99, 100, 101, 102, 103
CCRA.L.2	Demonstrate command of the conventions of standard English capitalization, punctuation, and spelling when writing.	104, 105, 106, 107, 108, 109
Knowledge of Language		
CCRA.L.3	Apply knowledge of language to understand how language functions in different contexts, to make effective choices for meaning or style, and to comprehend more fully when reading or listening.	110, 111, 112
Vocabulary Acquisition and Use		
CCRA.L.4	Determine or clarify the meaning of unknown and multiple-meaning words and phrases by using context clues, analyzing meaningful word parts, and consulting general and specialized reference materials, as appropriate.	113, 114, 115, 116, 117, 118, 119, 120, 121, 122, 123, 124, 125, 126
CCRA.L.5	Demonstrate understanding of figurative language, word relationships, and nuances in word meanings.	120, 121, 122
CCRA.L.6	Acquire and use accurately a range of general academic and domain-specific words and phrases sufficient for reading, writing, speaking, and listening at the college and career readiness level; demonstrate independence in gathering vocabulary knowledge when encountering an unknown term important to comprehension or expression.	126

Language Standards for Grade 5

Standard Number	Standard	Pages that Support
Conventions of Standard English		
L.5.1	Demonstrate command of the conventions of standard English grammar and usage when writing or speaking.	98-103
L.5.1a	Explain the function of conjunctions, prepositions, and interjections in general and their function in particular sentences.	98, 99, 100
L.5.1b	Form and use the perfect (e.g., *I had walked; I have walked; I will have walked*) verb tenses.	101
L.5.1c	Use verb tense to convey various times, sequences, states, and conditions.	101, 102, 103
L.5.1d	Recognize and correct inappropriate shifts in verb tense.	103
L.5.1e	Use correlative conjunctions (e.g., *either/or, neither/nor*).	98
L.5.2	Demonstrate command of the conventions of standard English capitalization, punctuation, and spelling when writing.	104-109
L.5.2a	Use punctuation to separate items in a series.	104, 105
L.5.2b	Use a comma to separate an introductory element from the rest of the sentence.	104, 105
L.5.2c	Use a comma to set off the words *yes* and *no* (e.g., *Yes, thank you*), to set off a tag question from the rest of the sentence (e.g., *It's true, isn't it?*), and to indicate direct address (e.g., *Is that you, Steve?*)	104, 105
L.5.2d	Use underlining, quotation marks, or italics to indicate titles of works.	106
L.5.2e	Spell grade-appropriate words correctly, consulting references as needed.	107, 108, 109

Language standards continue on next page.

Language Standards for Grade 5, continued

Standard Number	Standard	Pages that Support
Knowledge of Language		
L.5.3	Use knowledge of language and its conventions when writing, speaking, reading, or listening.	98-112
L.5.3a	Expand, combine, and reduce sentences for meaning, reader/listener interest, and style.	110, 111
L.5.3b	Compare and contrast the varieties of English (e.g., *dialects, registers*) used in stories, dramas, or poems.	*Apply this standard to oral demonstrations and discussions.*
L.5.3c	Differentiate between contexts that call for formal English (e.g., presenting ideas) and situations where informal discourse is appropriate (e.g., small-group discussion).	112
Vocabulary Acquisition and Use		
L.5.4	Determine or clarify the meaning of unknown and multiple-meaning words and phrases based on grade 5 reading and content, choosing flexibly from a range of strategies.	113-119
L.5.4a	Use context (e.g., cause/effect relationships and comparisons in text) as a clue to the meaning of a word or phrase.	113, 114, 115, 116, 117, 118, 119, 120, 121, 122, 123, 124, 125, 126
L.5.4b	Use common, grade-appropriate Greek and Latin affixes and roots as clues to the meaning of a word (e.g., *photograph, photosynthesis*).	116, 117
L.5.4c	Consult reference materials (e.g., dictionaries, glossaries, thesauruses), both print and digital, to find the pronunciation and determine or clarify the precise meaning of key words and phrases.	118, 119
L.5.5	Demonstrate understanding of figurative language, word relationships, and nuances in word meanings.	120-126
L.5.5a	Interpret figurative language, including similes and metaphors, in context.	120, 121, 122
L.5.5b	Recognize and explain the meaning of common idioms, adages, and proverbs.	120, 121, 122
L.5.5c	Use the relationship between particular words (e.g., synonyms, antonyms, homographs) to better understand each of the words.	123, 124, 125, 126
L.5.6	Acquire and use accurately grade-appropriate general academic and domain-specific words and phrases, including those that signal contrast, addition, and other logical relationships (e.g., *however, although, nevertheless, similarly, moreover, in addition*).	126

READING

LITERATURE

Grade 5

ADVENTURES UNLIMITED

Let us take you on the adventure of your dreams. *Adventures Unlimited* is the place to shop for any kind of travel! We'll take you to real or fantasy locations in the past, present, or future. Choose your adventure—and start packing!

Global EXUBERANCE

passport Explore beautiful soar

Travel new Wonders

TIME-TRAVEL ADVENTURES

Attend a masked ball at Versailles.
Learn to make a mummy in ancient Egypt.
Take a gander at Camelot.
Comb the streams for gold with the '49ers.
Test-drive a car of the future!
Drop in on Leonardo da Vinci.
Hang out at a Stone Age Rock Concert.
Rock with music groups of the far future.

EXPEDITIONS INTO WIND & WATER

Ride the world's most colossal waves.
Snoop around the ruins of the *Titanic*.
Raft through treacherous whitewater.

be...

Different

LITER...

customs

FANTASY ADVENTURES

Fraternize with the real Mother Goose.
Make friends with Paul Bunyan.
Try wild escapades with Pecos Bill.
Scrutinize clues with the legendary Sherlock Holmes.
Take a ride in Elvis's lavish Rolls Royce.

...rtune
tickets Magic

acations Heart

Find a word on one of the posters that matches the instructions below.
Look on both pages 22 and 23.

Find a word or phrase that means . . .

1. adventures _____

2. sail _____

3. tricks _____

4. socialize _____

5. examine _____

6. try _____

7. travel _____

Find two synonyms for *search*.

8. _____

_____

Find a word or phrase that means . . .

9. make-believe _____

10. grand _____

11. having to do with food _____

12. climb _____

Use with page 23.

Name

Space **DREAM**
MOUNTAIN
Fabulous
OUTRAGEOUS EXPEDITIONS
Take off on an escapade to the Mir Space Station.
Camp alone in the dark, foreboding forest.
Endeavor to climb the Empire State Building.

IMAGINE. **EXUBERANCE**
GREAT

BARGAIN ADVENTURES
Rule the court for a day.
Learn to soar through the air on a pole.
Eat your way to a culinary world record.

Modern

vacation

QUEST   Echoes

Creature Escapades!
Catch an elusive leprechaun.
Face the fiercest bull.
Search for a mythical mermaid.

REAL EXCITEMENT IN REAL PLACES
Probe the world's deepest cavern.
Spend a month at Clown College.
Learn downhill antics from Olympic champions.
Scale the great Denali Mountain.
Sail the highest, wildest seas.
Compete in the Iditarod.
Helicopter to ski the remote Alps.
Engage a ride on the Orient Express.

mother nature
perfect

GREAT MYSTERY ADVENTURES
Search for the lost city of Atlantis.
Venture into the Bermuda Triangle, if you dare.
Meet the unfathomable Loch Ness Monster.

Holy Cow!

**Find a word on one of the posters that matches the instructions below.
Look on both pages 22 and 23.**

Write a word that is an antonym for . . .

13. safe_____

14. real_____

15. modern _____

16. pleasant _____

17. small_____

18. plain and simple_____

19. understandable_____

20. past _____

Write a word that is a synonym for . . .

21. hard to catch _____

22. famous _____

23. wreck _____

24. a good price _____

25. hire_____

26. a look _____

27. far away _____

28. scariest _____

Use with page 22.

Name

Common Core Reinforcement Activities: 5th Grade Language

EXPLORE A DEEP CAVE

ADVENTURE #1 Explore the Réseau Jean Bernard Cave, one of the deepest caves in the world. Bring a hard hat, wear a raincoat, and don't forget the lights!

Find each of the words 1 to 12 in one of the speech balloons.
Write what the word means in that sentence.

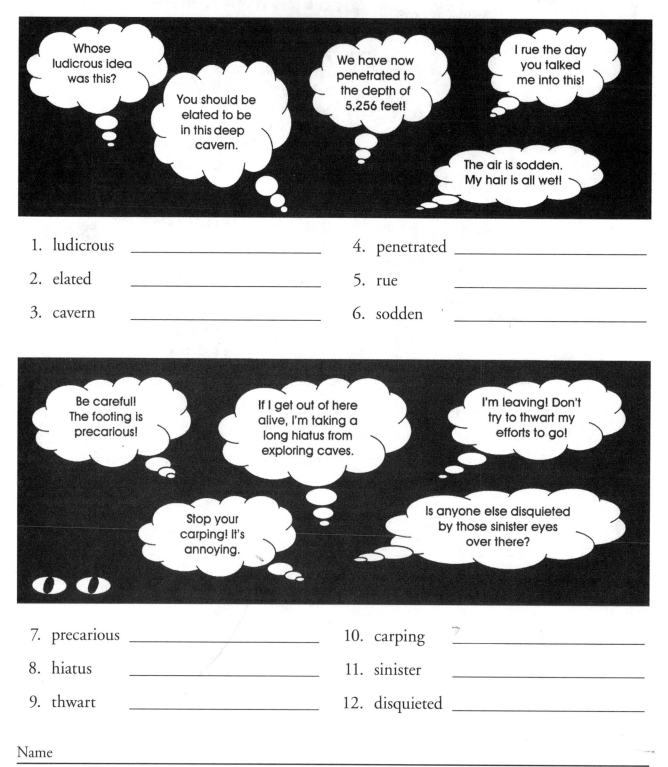

1. ludicrous _____

2. elated _____

3. cavern _____

4. penetrated _____

5. rue _____

6. sodden _____

7. precarious _____

8. hiatus _____

9. thwart _____

10. carping _____

11. sinister _____

12. disquieted _____

Name _____

TEST-DRIVE A COOL CAR

ADVENTURE #2 We'll sneak you into the secret showroom of one of the top car companies to see some cars of the future. Then you can hop right into the car of your choice and take it for a test drive!

Read the rules for test-driving this awesome vehicle. Write the meaning for each word listed at the bottom. Decide its meaning from the way it is used in the list of rules.

RULES for TEST-DRIVERS

#1 Drivers must certify that they are over age 10.

#2 Never render body safety restraints inoperable.

#3 Submit to all instructions given by the computer.

#4 Do not deploy parachutes at speeds under 70 mph.

#5 No ingesting of liquids at speeds over 200 mph.

#6 Do not eat pizza or other lardaceous foods in the car.

#7 Do not deposit or throw refuse in the car.

#8 Drivers are precluded from watching the movie system.

#9 Attend to information disseminated by the computer.

#10 This model is banned from the monorail systems.

#11 Do not tamper with automatic speed control devices.

#12 Drivers showing excessive aggression will be chastened.

#13 Any traffic citations will be charged to the driver.

#14 This car must be promptly returned at termination of drive.

PLEASE WEAR GLOVES WHEN TOUCHING MK 2020

MODEL K 2020

1. certify _____

2. render _____

   inoperable _____

3. submit _____

4. deploy _____

5. ingesting _____

6. lardaceous _____

7. refuse _____

8. precluded _____

9. attend _____

   disseminated _____

10. banned _____

11. tamper _____

12. excessive _____

    chastened _____

13. citations _____

14. promptly _____

    termination _____

Name _____

Common Core Reinforcement Activities: 5th Grade Language

MEET A GREAT ARTIST

ADVENTURE #3 Grab a seat on the time machine and head back to the Italian Renaissance to meet Leonardo da Vinci, an incredibly talented artist and scientist.

Answer the questions. Circle the part of a letter that supports your answer. Use the color indicated.

Venice, April 1509

Dear Leonardo,

I have been a fan of yours for years. You are a remarkable man. I am so impressed with your paintings, the *Mona Lisa*, which you painted in Florence in early 1503, and *The Last Supper*, which you painted earlier in Milan. Why did you never finish your painting of St. Jerome? I wish I could meet you.

Giorgio

Florence, May 1507

Dear Leonardo,
I am so impressed with your notebooks, where you put the most important information into your drawings. I hear there are thousands of pages. They are full of amazing drawings and notes about painting, architecture, human anatomy, mechanics, biology, and other things. When did you have time to write them all?

Alicia

Chicago, June 1998
Dear Leonardo,
I am surprised to learn that you drew plans for an airplane and a helicopter centuries before flying machines were successfully built. I have also been amazed to see your perfect drawings of human anatomy. I always thought you were only an artist! But now I have learned that you were also a scientist, sculptor, architect, mathematician, military advisor, and engineer!

charlie

1. RED ....Which letter mentions an unfinished painting? _____

2. BLUE...........What surprised Charlie?_____

3. GREEN ....What was in Leonardo's notebooks?_____

4. BLACK........What art skills (other than painting) are mentioned?_____

_____

5. YELLOW .....Was the *Mona Lisa* or the *Last Supper* finished first?_____

6. ORANGE.....Which letter focused on Leonardo's paintings?_____

Name _____

DINE WITH THE FORTY-NINERS

ADVENTURE #4 Search for gold with the Forty-Niners! Travel back to 1849 when the Gold Rush was in full swing in Northern California. Maybe you'll be one of the fortunate adventurers and end up with a pan full of golden nuggets!

Camp cook Gus Grubb has great recipes. But they are all out of order.

Read them carefully, and number the steps in the correct sequence. Join with one or more classmates to explain your choices.

GOLDEN NUGGET STEW

___ Then cook them in hot chicken fat in a big kettle.
___ First, cut up 5 chickens into small nuggets.
___ Sprinkle with red pepper flakes before serving.
___ Cook for 1 more hour.
___ Roll the nuggets in flour mixed with salt and mustard powder.
___ When the chicken is tender, throw in many handfuls of cut-up carrots, turnips, onions, and potatoes.

HEARTY CORN BREAD

___ Add 5 cups of whole wheat flour to the starter.
___ Finally, stir in some chunks of cheese.
___ Toss 1 cup of baking powder into the flour and cornmeal mixture.
___ Next, mix in 5 cups of corn meal in with the flour and starter.
___ Bake over a hot fire until it's brown on top.
___ Start with ½ cup of sourdough starter.
___ Sprinkle kernels of corn on top of the mixture.
___ Pour the mixture into a pan.

GREAT-CAMPOUT GRUB

___ Boil the hambone in 2 gallons of water for 3 hours.
___ After the beans, add your favorite spices.
___ Serve with hot corn bread.
___ Start with a big old hambone.
___ The second ingredient is 10 cans of beans— loads of fat, white beans.
___ Cook for 1 hour over a hot camp fire.
___ During the last 20 minutes of cooking, add 2 cups of sliced carrots.

My number one secret ingredient is...

Catsup!

Name _____

Common Core Reinforcement Activities: 5th Grade Language

ROCK INTO THE PAST

ADVENTURE #5 Attend the very first rock concert! Take an awesome time-machine ride into the Stone Age and get ready to rock.

Use information from the poster to answer the questions.

1. Who performs *My Cave's on Fire?*

2. What comes just before the intermission?

3. What song does Mick Jagged & the Rolling Boulders perform?

4. Which song is performed by Curt McCave?

5. Who sings with Bronto?

6. What do the Limestone Lovers perform?

7. Who is the lead singer with the Hot Rocks?

8. Who performs *The Gravel Pit Rock?*

9. Who sings about a brontosaurus?

10. Where is the concert held?

11. What song does Tommy Shale perform?

12. When does the concert begin?

13. Who sings about granite?

Name

GRANITEVILLE MUSIC FEST
Place: Hard Rock Arena
Time: After Dark

PROGRAM

I Dino If I Love You Anymore
Mick Jagged & the Rolling Boulders

I Feel Like a Brontosaurus Stomped on My Head
The Petro Cliff Trio

Your Love Is Like a Sabre-Tooth Tiger
Terri Dactyl & the Hot Rocks

Sha-boom, Sha-boom, Sha-Rock
The Lava-Ettes

You're As Cuddly As a Woolly Mammoth
The Smashing Marbles

INTERMISSION

Be a Little Boulder, Honey
Curt McCave

The Gravel Pit Rock
The Cro-Magnon Crooners

Please Don't Take Me for Granite, Baby
The Standing Stones

My Cave's on Fire
The Paleo-Lyths

Your Heart's Made of Stone
Bronto & the Cave Dudes

Dancin' at the Quarry
Tommy Shale

I've Cried Pebbles over You
The Limestone Lovers

Till the Volcano Blows
The Square Wheels

RIDE THE HIGH SEAS

ADVENTURE #6 Have you always wanted to get your hands on the wheel and try to steer a ship at sea? Here's your chance to be the captain of a sailing vessel. Let's hope you don't get seasick!

Use the color indicated to circle parts of the text to answer each question. Be ready to discuss your choices.

The Terror of the Wind
by Tahli O., Gr. 3

The sea was roaring up with thunder
Up to the angry winds,
Which tore through the air dancing to and fro.
Once again the lightning slipped another cut into
    the dancing air,
Which wailed and wailed from the lightning sharp knife.
The sea kept moaning from the mountains that rose
    higher and higher as they crawled upon its back,
And again the thunder crashed through the air, trying
    to hide itself from the pounding rain,
As it poured through the air.
Then after all its strikes, the lightning's knife grew dull,
As it stabbed the sea once more.
Then the sea could no longer hold the towering mountains
    upon its back.
As the rain grew tired of falling,
It carefully settled down to rest,
As the thunder rolled back up to the sky to sleep for the night.
The wind's feet could not take another step,
As tired as it was,
The wind could not say another word,
As one last drop of water fell from the sky,
And landed on the top of the sea, to settle down to sleep in
The dark coldness of the night.

1. How does the author convey the visual images of lightning? (Circle phrases or words in YELLOW.)

2. What actions of the sea are described? (Circle in BLUE.)

3. What words suggest that the lightning is alive? (Underline in RED.)

4. What words suggest the winds are alive? (Underline in ORANGE.)

5. How do you know the wind became tired? (Circle in GREEN.)

6. How do you know the sea became tired? (Circle in PURPLE.)

Name

Copyright © 2014 World Book, Inc./
Incentive Publications, Chicago, IL

Common Core Reinforcement Activities: 5th Grade Language

JOIN THE CIRCUS!

ADVENTURE #7 Many people fantasize about running away to join the circus. If you are not afraid of heights or tigers, this is just the right adventure for you. (Do you have a great sense of balance? That will surely help!)

A proverb is a short, wise saying that communicates some truthful idea. Read these proverbs. Think about them as they could relate to the illustration.

1. What theme do these sayings have in common?

   _____

   _____

   _____

   _____

2. Write a brief summary of the message or messages given by all the proverbs taken together. Relate the summary to the illustration.

   _____

   _____

   _____

   _____

   _____

   _____

   _____

   _____

Name _____

RIDE THE *ORIENT EXPRESS*

ADVENTURE #8 It's the famous train of luxury and mystery. Ride the *Orient Express* from Paris to Istanbul. Keep your eyes open for unusual events! This trip is anything but ordinary.

SOMETHING IS STRANGE ON THE ORIENT EXPRESS

Madeline Merry wanders around to explore the train. This is her first trip on the *Orient Express*. She looks like an innocent child playing in the aisles, yet she loves to play detective. She is really out snooping. As she passes the countess, she notices that the little dog has a small packet mostly hidden beneath his neck. Her watchful eye does not miss the countess slipping something into the doctor's open bag as she squeezes past him in the aisle. Next, Madeline knows that the man in the berth is snoring, but why are his eyes peeking out from beneath mostly closed lids? He does not seem to care that a sneaky fellow is reaching out for his watch.

Madeline plays with her yo-yo, but her ears do not miss the whispering behind a closed curtain. Nor can she ignore the large lump in the pocket of the proper-looking Mrs. Matisse. Why is Mrs. Matisse hovering awfully close to the mysterious man who hides behind his collar? And what is in the package she is guarding so closely?

As Madeline roams along the aisle, the train suddenly jerks to a stop. Baggage and people fly everywhere, and then the lights go out. There is much squealing and screaming in the dark. When the lights are turned back on, the woman who claims to be a countess is screeching, "My doggie! My doggie! Someone has taken my doggie!" As passengers are scurrying around, Madeline sees that the doctor's bag is on the shelf and another bag is in his hand. Mrs. Matisse has lost her hat, and the porter is missing. Just then, Madeline's mother comes and grabs her by the hand. It is time for her family to leave the train.

Follow the directions below.

1. Briefly describe the theme of the story.

   _____

   _____

   _____

2. Write a brief summary of the story.

   _____

   _____

   _____

   _____

   _____

Name _____

FOLLOW CLUES WITH SHERLOCK

ADVENTURE #9 Track down clues and solve crimes with the world's most famous detective, Sherlock Holmes.

Snoop into Sherlock's detective log to see his current cases. Read the outline, and write a short summary of each case so far.

Case #1   Mrs. McCurty's Missing Jewels

Jewels are stolen at 8 P.M. Friday from dresser drawer.
Suspects:

Nanny Opal: did not come to work Saturday
　　　Her sister and doctor say she is sick.
Grandma Ruby: stays locked in her room
　　　She has taken the jewels before.
The Butler: has bulging pockets
　　　He is angry at his employer for refusing a pay raise.
Neighbor, Professor Gem: recently put a large sum into his bank account
　　　He is really Simon Topaz, previously arrested for jewel theft.

Case Summary: _____

_____

_____

Case #2   The Missing Raw Meat

Butcher reports 22 pounds of raw meat missing, Saturday midnight.
Suspects:

Count Janson's cat: has an extended belly
Brewster's dog: has stolen meat several times before,
　　　has a satisfied look on his face on Sunday, raw meat on his paws
Cook at la Mancha Hotel: served beef rolls Sunday,
　　　was out of town until Sunday morning at 6 A.M.
Garbage Collector: seen digging through Butcher's trash

Case Summary: _____

_____

_____

Case #3   Broken Lamppost on Canterbury Lane

- Yellow paint found on bent lamppost Wednesday night;
  broken glass on ground from burst lamp
- Talked to all homeowners in the area
- Checked all carriage repair shops
- Checked with shops selling yellow paint
- Found names of owners of seven yellow carriages

Case Summary: _____

_____

_____

Name _____

NAVIGATE A RAGING RIVER

ADVENTURE #10 There's no thrill quite like a whitewater thrill!
Travel to Costa Rica to take on some breathtaking rapids.
If you know how to swim, we'll provide the wet suit
and plenty of thrills—hopefully, with no spills!

I got through the rapids by the skin of my teeth!

I got through those rapids by the skin of my teeth.

The whirlpool kept shouting, "I'll pull you beneath."

"We dare you to crash!" call the rocks up ahead.

The current calls out, "I am what you dread."

The voices get louder the further I go.

Is the river against me? Is the water my foe?

What grudge does it hold? What have I done?

Can the rivalry end? Or can I go on?

Follow the directions below.

1. Identify the theme of the poem.

   _____

   _____

   _____

2. Write a brief summary of the poem.

   _____

   _____

   _____

   _____

   _____

   _____

   _____

Name _____

Common Core Reinforcement Activities: 5th Grade Language

VISIT A GRAND PALACE

ADVENTURE #11 Find yourself a great costume and a wonderful mask. You're invited to be the guest of King Louis XIV at the great palace of Versailles!

On this page and the next page (page 35), read about each guest you will meet at the ball. Then answer the questions.

Count Pompous is strutting about the great hall with a fancy hat and his high-heeled boots. He will probably keep his nose in the air the entire evening.

Countess Dainté dances lightly across the ballroom floor. She seems to float around the room with a light step. Everything about her seems soft, sweet, and sincere.

1. How do the characters of Count Pompous and Countess Dainté differ?

   _____

   _____

   _____

   _____

   Circle the words or phrases that support your answer.

2. How is Jacques like Prince Mischief? (See page 35.)

   _____

   _____

   _____

   _____

   _____

   What a jolly fellow is the friendly Jacques Joli! It's a pleasure to have his company. He has a clever, happy word for every guest.

   Circle the words or phrases that support your answer.

Use with page 35.

Name

Character, Setting, Events

Read about these guests, too. Then answer the questions.

3. What other guest is Lady Columbine most like?

_____

Lady Columbine is busy showing off her beauty and grace. She just knows that everyone is looking at her and no one else. If you are not a young, handsome, wealthy prince, she won't want to waste her time on you!

What information from the text led to this conclusion?

_____

_____

_____

Little Prince Mischief just loves these parties, too! He is so small that guests hardly notice him. He lurks around under tables and behind curtains, having loads of fun!

4. How is Prince Mischief different from Dowager La-de-da?

_____

_____

_____

_____

Circle the words or phrases that support your answer.

5. What advice might Judge d'Éclaire give to Lady Columbine?

_____

_____

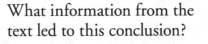

What information from the text led to this conclusion?

_____

_____

_____

_____

There's Dowager La-de-da! How honored you should be to come into the presence of this rich old dame. Be sure you do not say anything rowdy or improper in her presence. She has no time for foolishness.

Judge d'Éclaire is a very important man. He loves these parties because of the plentiful food. Oh, how he loves to eat! If you stop to visit with him, do bring him a pastry or two.

Use with page 34.

Name

Common Core Reinforcement Activities: 5th Grade Language

BE A JUDGE FOR THE DAY

ADVENTURE #12 It's just what you've always wanted! This week, **you** get to be the judge. Take over Judge Weary's courtroom and decide the cases yourself. The black robe and gavel will be provided.

Read the facts provided for each case. Then write your judgment. Join with one or more classmates to tell how the written facts affected your decision. Tell what you (the judge) will order to settle each issue.

CASE #1   The Deceased Cat

Miss LaGrady claims that her neighbor killed her cat. She found the cat dead on her doorstep, with traces of slimy green bologna on its whiskers and paws. Remains of the same bologna were found in the garbage can of her next door neighbor, Mr. Clam. Should Mr. Clam pay for the cat's burial and Miss LaGrady's grief counseling?

Your judgment _____

CASE #2   Neighbors vs The Magenta Family

The entire neighborhood association is suing the Magenta Family for disrupting the neighborhood. They claim that the purple spots that the Magentas painted on their house are an eyesore. They say the awful color drives home buyers away. They have asked that the Magentas be forced to repaint their house and pay each neighbor a sum of $1,000.

Your judgment _____

CASE #3   The Potato Chip Deceit

Mr. Port claims that the Crunchy Potato Chip Company is responsible for his gain of 100 pounds. He points out that the potato chip bag says that the chips contain 200 calories. He thought that meant 200 calories per bag, so he ate a bag every day for two years. When he gained so much weight, he became suspicious of the chips and had them analyzed. The truth is, the chips contain 200 calories per serving. That adds up to 2,000 per bag. Should the company pay Mr. Port $3,000 to go to a weight loss program?

Your judgment _____

Name _____

CATCH A LEPRECHAUN

ADVENTURE #13 Travel with us to the land of magic. Visit Ireland and hunt for those friendly little elves called *leprechauns*. Catch one (if you can)! Maybe you'll find a pot of gold while you're searching!

With magic you can soar into the clouds with the angels,

Say hello to the fairies and play tag with lightning,

Fly on winged unicorns' backs,

Go to the Amazon Jungle and play with boas and black panthers,

Be a wizard, a super hero, a monster, or almost anything else,

Smell the prehistoric air, create a time machine, go to the future,

Build a giant hunk of metal into a star-ship,

Be the first girl or boy to dig to the pit of the earth,

Pull a bunny out of your hat,

Glide from the stars,

And slide down bright, colorful rainbows.

Wherever you are, whatever time it is,

You can find magic in your heart

And be anything,

And do anything you want to do!

Paul I., Gr 4

Use the passage on the mushroom to answer the questions.

1. How would you describe the structure of this poem? (Think about the way the writer presents the ideas.)

   _____

   _____

   _____

   _____

   _____

   _____

2. What is the effect of this structure on the message, tone, or feel of the poem?

   _____

   _____

   _____

   _____

   _____

Name _____

Common Core Reinforcement Activities: 5th Grade Language

SEE YOUR NAME IN LIGHTS

ADVENTURE #14 Take a trip with us down to the home of country music, Nashville, Tennessee. Live your dream of performing at the Grand Ole Opry! Maybe you'll even become a star!

Read these paragraphs about hopeful musicians getting their names in lights. (Read on this page and page 39.) Identify the point of view and author's purpose for each one.

1. How exciting to see Talula's name in lights! She's been a'singin' her heart out since she was just an itsy, bitsy girl. I watched her make a pretend microphone from her mama's egg beater when she was just knee-high to a dinner table. She just stood there and belted out the tune "Your Cheatin' Heart" at the top of her little lungs. If anyone deserves to be a big star—it's Talula.

Who's telling the story? (Circle one.)
  a. a character in the story
  b. a narrator who is not in the story
  c. a narrator who is a character in the story

What is the author's purpose?

_____

_____

_____

What information from the text helped you decide the purpose?

_____

_____

_____

2. I headed for Nashville at age 16 with my guitar over my shoulder and a song in my head. I planned to be a star. Ten years later, without a dollar to my name and no hit songs, I headed out of town. Everyone in Nashville wants to be a star. I heard "No, thanks" a thousand times. No one wanted my singin', my song writin', or my guitar playin'. This is a town that'll break your heart and your bank account.

Who's telling the story? (Circle one.)
  a. a character in the story
  b. a narrator who is not in the story
  c. a narrator who is a character in the story

What is the author's purpose?

_____

_____

What information from the text helped you decide the purpose?

_____

_____

_____

Use with page 39.

Name _____

Read these paragraphs about hopeful musicians getting their names in lights. Identify the point of view and author's purpose for each one.

NEWS FLASH!!

3. Rising star James T. Twang has a new hit. His song "**You've Broken My Phone, My Computer, and My Heart**" leaped to the top of the Country Music Charts last week. This is good news for a hometown boy.

Who's telling the story? (Circle one.)
   a. a character in the story
   b. a narrator who is not in the story
   c. a narrator who is a character in the story

What is the author's purpose?

_____

_____

What information from the text helped you decide the purpose?

_____

_____

IT'S A GAS!

4. Every time you see those brilliant colored lights, you'll know that they are made with gas. A French scientist, Georges Claude, figured out how to take rare gases out of the atmosphere and put them into tubes. An electric spark is sent streaking through the tubes. Different gases give off different colors as the spark goes through them, so different gases are put in the tubes to create different colors. Other colors are made by using tubes that are tinted or coated with certain powders that give off a colored glow. When someone's name lights up in neon, this is how it happens!

Who's telling the story? (Circle one.)
   a. a character in the story
   b. a narrator who is not in the story
   c. a narrator who is a character in the story

What is the author's purpose?

_____

_____

What information from the text helped you decide the purpose?

_____

_____

Use with page 38.

Name _____

Common Core Reinforcement Activities: 5th Grade Language

CATCH A BIG WAVE

ADVENTURE #15 In *big wave surfing*, surfers paddle
or are towed into waves that are at least 20 feet (6 meters) high.

Head out to the north shore of Oahu, Hawaii,
to catch a big one. Be careful! Don't wipe out!
A breaking wave can push you
many feet below the water.

A watery monster, rising, climbing, surging toward sky, now folds, rolls, and curls under itself --- Wrapping around spray, seaweed, and surfer, it plunges on its circular path and digs back into itself, leaving only a foamy reminder that it ever was...

Let your eye catch the full impact of this unusual text as you read the passage. Then answer the questions.

1. How does the look of the text affect the meaning or communication of the idea?

   _____

   _____

   _____

2. What words or phrases add to the idea shown by the shape?

   _____

   _____

   _____

Name

PREPARE TO SAY "WOW!"

ADVENTURE #16 Boston, Massachusetts, has become one of the best places to watch fireworks on July Fourth. Each year, the city pulls out all the stops with an extravagant show over the Charles River. You can be there! Sign up now!

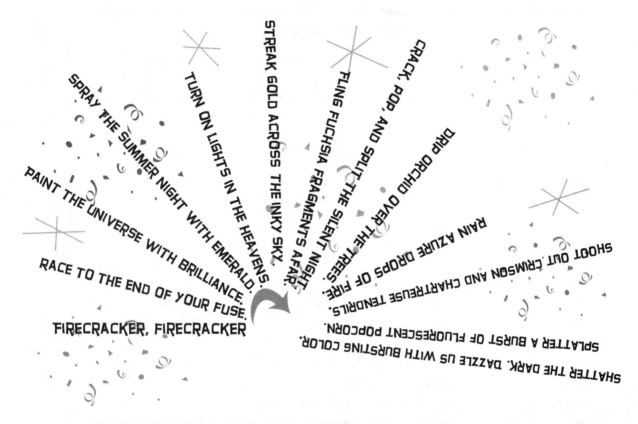

Let your eye catch the full impact of this unusual text as you read the passage. Then answer the questions.

1. How does the look of the text affect the meaning or communication of the idea?

   _____

   _____

   _____

2. What words or phrases add to the idea shown by the shape?

   _____

   _____

   _____

Name _____

Common Core Reinforcement Activities: 5th Grade Language

TAKE A DARING RIDE

ADVENTURE #17 Be one of the first to ride the *Scream Machine*! It's a huge, new, twisty, terrifying roller coaster. Don't choose this adventure unless you have a stomach of iron.

THIRTEEN THRILLS on THIRTEEN HILLS

You have waited in line for two hours to ride the new upside-down, triple-loop, heart-stopping roller coaster. It has thirteen awesome hills. While you wait, you begin to imagine the screams and screeches you'll soon be hearing.

You are nervous, excited, impatient to get on. You trust this roller coaster, or you wouldn't be trying it out. Even though you're the first customer to ride, you are sure it will be safe. When it's time to ride, you don't care how it works. You just want to get on!

A moving chain will pull the car to the top. When the car gets to the peak of the hill and starts to tip toward the other side, gravity pulls it down the steep slope. At the very top of each hill, your body keeps going up out of your seat because of inertia. You feel like you are flying, but soon gravity has you back in your seat again. At every curve and every upside-down loop, centripetal force pushes you against your seat. This is why you don't fall out. Finally, friction slows down the coaster and stops it.

The ride is over. You enjoyed every minute of it. Your stomach feels great, and you want to ride again right away!

Go on to read the poem about the *Scream Machine* on the next page (page 43). Then answer the questions to compare the two texts.

1. How does the structure of text of "Thirteen Thrills on Thirteen Hills" differ from that of "Only for the Brave and Bold," the poem on the next page?

   _____

   _____

2. How does the content of the two texts differ?

   _____

   _____

3. What is similar about the two texts?

   _____

   _____

Use with page 43.

Name

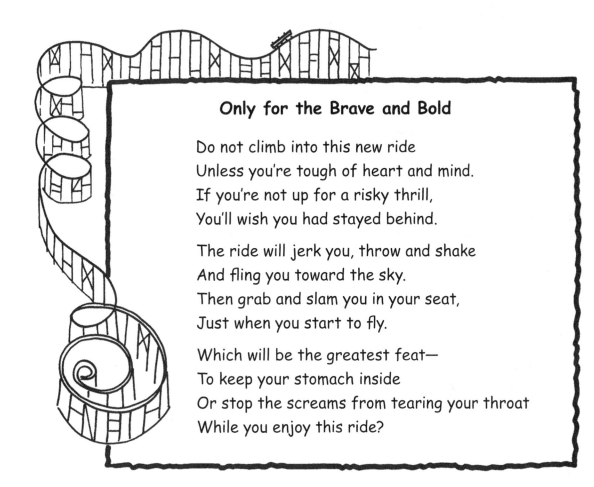

Only for the Brave and Bold

Do not climb into this new ride
Unless you're tough of heart and mind.
If you're not up for a risky thrill,
You'll wish you had stayed behind.

The ride will jerk you, throw and shake
And fling you toward the sky.
Then grab and slam you in your seat,
Just when you start to fly.

Which will be the greatest feat—
To keep your stomach inside
Or stop the screams from tearing your throat
While you enjoy this ride?

**Read the text on page 42 along with this poem.
Then answer the questions to compare the two texts.**

4. How does the author's purpose for "Only for the Brave and Bold" compare to the author's purpose for "Thirteen Thrills on Thirteen Hills"?

_____

_____

_____

5. How does the structure of each text affect its tone or message?

_____

_____

_____

_____

Use with page 42.

Name _____

READ SOME NEW OLD NEWS

ADVENTURE #18 Drop into a world where an old nursery rhyme turns into today's headline.

The story of Jack Sprat and his wife is a famous nursery rhyme. Read the story in some different forms. Be ready to discuss the similarities and differences between the forms and the way each form affects the mood or message.

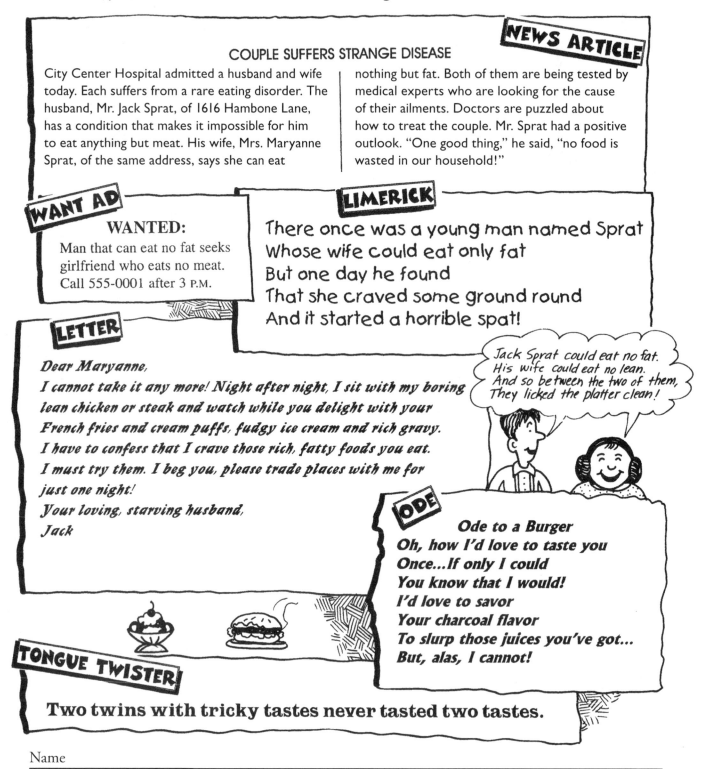

NEWS ARTICLE

COUPLE SUFFERS STRANGE DISEASE

City Center Hospital admitted a husband and wife today. Each suffers from a rare eating disorder. The husband, Mr. Jack Sprat, of 1616 Hambone Lane, has a condition that makes it impossible for him to eat anything but meat. His wife, Mrs. Maryanne Sprat, of the same address, says she can eat nothing but fat. Both of them are being tested by medical experts who are looking for the cause of their ailments. Doctors are puzzled about how to treat the couple. Mr. Sprat had a positive outlook. "One good thing," he said, "no food is wasted in our household!"

WANT AD

WANTED:

Man that can eat no fat seeks girlfriend who eats no meat. Call 555-0001 after 3 P.M.

LIMERICK

There once was a young man named Sprat
Whose wife could eat only fat
But one day he found
That she craved some ground round
And it started a horrible spat!

LETTER

Dear Maryanne,
I cannot take it any more! Night after night, I sit with my boring lean chicken or steak and watch while you delight with your French fries and cream puffs, fudgy ice cream and rich gravy. I have to confess that I crave those rich, fatty foods you eat. I must try them. I beg you, please trade places with me for just one night!
Your loving, starving husband,
Jack

Jack Sprat could eat no fat.
His wife could eat no lean.
And so between the two of them,
They licked the platter clean!

ODE

Ode to a Burger
Oh, how I'd love to taste you
Once...If only I could
You know that I would!
I'd love to savor
Your charcoal flavor
To slurp those juices you've got...
But, alas, I cannot!

TONGUE TWISTER

Two twins with tricky tastes never tasted two tastes.

Name _____

READING

INFORMATIONAL TEXT

Grade 5

Hmmm, very interesting!

THE ULTIMATE GUIDE TO SLEUTHING

JOIN A SLEUTH ACADEMY

ADVENTURE #19 The detectives-in-training at the Super-Sleuth Academy are proud of their record. You, too, can learn how to solve such fascinating cases.

The detectives have recorded their successfully solved cases. Use the table to answer the questions.

Super–Sleuth Training Academy
SOLVED CASES: Class Group #3

Kinds of Cases	G. Ghastly	S. Snoop	G. Gumshoe	B. Sharp	L. Insee
Bank Robberies	1	23	24	0	1
Art Thefts	2	15	12	11	0
Missing Animals	3	25	19	16	22
Break-Ins	4	10	18	31	23
Stolen Cars	0	25	7	13	12
Jewelry Thefts	1	21	13	0	29
Paranormal Cases (Ghosts and Such)	27	1	0	4	0

1. Which detective has been most successful overall? _____
    How do you know? _____
    _____

2. What kinds of cases were least common? _____
    How do you know? _____
    _____

3. What kinds of cases were most common? _____
    How do you know? _____
    _____

4. What does Gary Gumshoe seem to do best? _____
    How do you know? _____
    _____

5. What would you say is Detective Ghastly's specialty? _____
    How do you know? _____
    _____

Use with page 47.

Name

CHECK OUT SOME CURIOUS CASES

ADVENTURE #20 Student detective Bea Sharp outlines her report on her cases. Get your feet wet at the Super-Sleuth Academy by reviewing her homework assignment. See what you can learn about her cases.

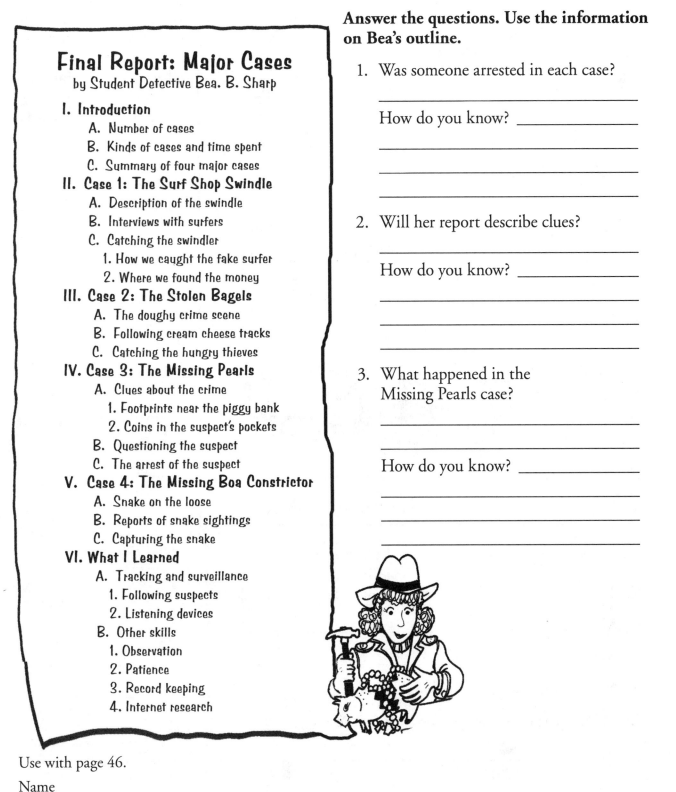

Final Report: Major Cases
by Student Detective Bea. B. Sharp

I. Introduction
   A. Number of cases
   B. Kinds of cases and time spent
   C. Summary of four major cases

II. Case 1: The Surf Shop Swindle
   A. Description of the swindle
   B. Interviews with surfers
   C. Catching the swindler
      1. How we caught the fake surfer
      2. Where we found the money

III. Case 2: The Stolen Bagels
   A. The doughy crime scene
   B. Following cream cheese tracks
   C. Catching the hungry thieves

IV. Case 3: The Missing Pearls
   A. Clues about the crime
      1. Footprints near the piggy bank
      2. Coins in the suspect's pockets
   B. Questioning the suspect
   C. The arrest of the suspect

V. Case 4: The Missing Boa Constrictor
   A. Snake on the loose
   B. Reports of snake sightings
   C. Capturing the snake

VI. What I Learned
   A. Tracking and surveillance
      1. Following suspects
      2. Listening devices
   B. Other skills
      1. Observation
      2. Patience
      3. Record keeping
      4. Internet research

Answer the questions. Use the information on Bea's outline.

1. Was someone arrested in each case?

   _____

   How do you know? _____

   _____

   _____

   _____

2. Will her report describe clues?

   _____

   How do you know? _____

   _____

   _____

   _____

3. What happened in the Missing Pearls case?

   _____

   _____

   How do you know? _____

   _____

   _____

   _____

Use with page 46.

Name _____

Common Core Reinforcement Activities: 5th Grade Language

LEARN TO MAKE A MUMMY

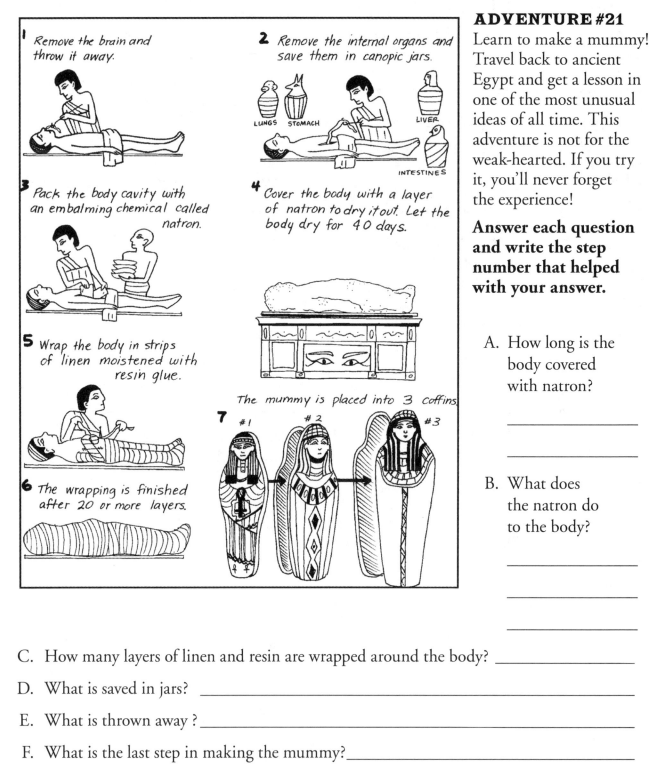

1 Remove the brain and throw it away.

2 Remove the internal organs and save them in canopic jars.

LUNGS   STOMACH   LIVER   INTESTINES

3 Pack the body cavity with an embalming chemical called natron.

4 Cover the body with a layer of natron to dry it out. Let the body dry for 40 days.

5 Wrap the body in strips of linen moistened with resin glue.

6 The wrapping is finished after 20 or more layers.

The mummy is placed into 3 coffins.

7 #1   #2   #3

ADVENTURE #21

Learn to make a mummy! Travel back to ancient Egypt and get a lesson in one of the most unusual ideas of all time. This adventure is not for the weak-hearted. If you try it, you'll never forget the experience!

Answer each question and write the step number that helped with your answer.

A. How long is the body covered with natron?

_____

_____

B. What does the natron do to the body?

_____

_____

_____

C. How many layers of linen and resin are wrapped around the body? _____

D. What is saved in jars? _____

E. What is thrown away ? _____

F. What is the last step in making the mummy?_____

G. Which part of the process looks the hardest? _____

Tell why._____

Name

RACE WITH THE DOGS

ADVENTURE #22 Bring your warmest clothes to Alaska because you'll be driving a team of racing sled dogs over a snow-covered course! You might even get good enough to join the toughest race of all: the Iditarod Sled Dog Race®.

Read the weather reports for the first six days of the Iditarod. Then answer the questions below. Circle the part of the text that helps you answer each question.

DAY 1: WEATHER REPORT
The skies will be clear today, with temperatures at 0 °F (-18 °C). Light fluffy snow covers the ground.

DAY 2: WEATHER REPORT
Temperatures are warming. Expect a light rain, which will turn to freezing rain this afternoon.

DAY 3: WEATHER REPORT
Heavy fog will move in, bringing moist, wet air hovering over the snow. Winds will be harsh this evening

DAY 4: WEATHER REPORT
Extreme blizzard conditions are reported today. Warnings are out for complete white-out conditions. Winds are blowing at 60 mph (97 kph) with drifts up to six feet (two meters).

DAY 5: WEATHER REPORT
Today the temperatures will climb to 20 °F (-7 °C) with light snow showers and light winds.

DAY 6: WEATHER REPORT
Temperatures have taken a plunge. At noon, we recorded -25 °F (-32 °C) with a -80 °F (-62 °C) wind chill factor. Everyone is warned to stay indoors. It is extremely dangerous for people or animals to be outdoors in these conditions.

1. On what day might the conditions be slippery? _____

2. What day(s) might have the best conditions for racing? _____

3. What troubles might drivers and dogs have on Day 3? _____

   _____

4. On what days might visibility be a problem? _____

   _____

5. What would you expect the racing teams or race officials to do on Day 6? _____

   _____

   _____

Name _____

Common Core Reinforcement Activities: 5th Grade Language

EXPLORE THE SUNKEN *TITANIC*

ADVENTURE #23 Join the underwater explorers as they unlock the mysteries of this great ship, the *Titanic*.

Find the key idea in each paragraph. Write it on the lines. Then circle one important detail that supports the key idea.

THE VOYAGE OF THE *TITANIC*

They called it "unsinkable," but the *Titanic* was not. They called it a floating luxury hotel, and indeed it was! It was like a huge palace, with huge rooms, gold-plated light fixtures, a swimming pool, and steam baths. No ship this big or beautiful had ever been built before! Hundreds of passengers and families boarded the *Titanic* in Southampton, England, on April 10, 1912. The great new ship was bound for New York on its maiden voyage.

_____

_____

Late on the night of April 14, 1912, disaster struck the *Titanic*. Actually, the ship struck disaster—in the form of an iceberg. At first, passengers didn't realize that the accident was serious. There was a command for people to get into the lifeboats. Unfortunately, the company that built the boat was so convinced it was unsinkable that they had installed lifeboats for only about half the people on board.

_____

_____

The ship sent out distress signals, hoping nearby ships would come to help. The bow of the Titanic was sinking when a loud, roaring noise went up from the ship. The *Titanic* was breaking apart. It stood up in the air for a short while, and then disappeared beneath the waves. The next day, another ship, the *Carpathia*, came to rescue many survivors. Survivors included 712 passengers and crew members. Hundreds did not survive.

_____

_____

_____

There are many theories about why the *Titanic* sank. Seventy-five years after the sinking, and after much searching, the wreckage of the *Titanic* was found. Small submarines have explored the wreckage. Maybe some of the mysteries will now be solved.

_____

_____

_____

Name _____

SPECIALIZE IN SURVEILLANCE

ADVENTURE #24 Learn the art of surveillance. Luke Insee is a specialist. He's using a listening device to eavesdrop on the phone conversations of some crime suspects. Help him out.

Read each conversation. Circle key ideas or details that you read. Write a short summary of each conversation in Luke's notebook.

CONVERSATION 1 (Monday, 3 p.m.)

Sammy the Sneak to his Ma: "Hi, Ma. Did you send that special cake to Cousin Louie in the Big House yet?"

Ma: "I'm sorry, Son. My stove is broken. Can I send him the file in a submarine sandwich instead?"

CONVERSATION 2 (Monday, 4 p.m.)

Maxie Mayhem: "Here's the plan, Moll. We are going to meet the gang at midnight on Pier 15. And don't forget to bring the loot."

Moll: "I don't have the loot. You have the loot!"

Maxie: "Don't be silly. Of course you have the loot! It was your job to hide the loot . . ."

Moll: "Uh oh, someone's in big trouble now . . ."

CONVERSATION 3 (Tuesday, 7 p.m.)

Harry the Horse to Pete's Pizza Shop: "Bring the pizza in a plain brown wrapper to Fifth and Broadway and leave it behind the third garbage can on the corner. Make sure nobody sees you. Blow a dog whistle and wait for 20 seconds. Then, if everything is clear, the money will be lowered to you in a manila envelope. Got it?"

Pete: "Got it."

Harry: "And Pete, that pizza better be hot!"

CONVERSATION 4 (Thursday, noon)

Shorty: "We're ready to go for tomorrow. Have you got the getaway plan all set?"

Unidentified Voice: "Do you want me to rent a compact car or a luxury car?"

Shorty: "Are you nuts? You can't rent a car for a bank robbery! The police aren't stupid, you know!"

Voice: "Uh, I wasn't gonna give them my name. I plan to use your credit card."

Shorty: "No rentals! Got it?"

SUMMARIES

#1 _____

_____

_____

#2 _____

_____

_____

#3 _____

_____

_____

#4 _____

_____

Name _____

Common Core Reinforcement Activities: 5th Grade Language

HANG OUT WITH PAUL BUNYAN

ADVENTURE #25 Are all those stories about Paul Bunyan really true? Head off into the forest and meet him for yourself. Maybe he'll teach you how to swing an axe or how to eat 37 pancakes at one sitting!

JOB APPLICATION Position: LUMBERJACK	
Name	Paul Bunyan
Age	22
Place of Birth	Maine
Height	8 feet 11 inches (3 meters)
Weight	344 pounds (156 kilograms)
Physical Condition	EXCELLENT
Shoe Size	200 (700 European)
Experience	Woodsplitting, tree felling, lumberjack work across the nation
Abilities & Qualities That Make You Fit for the Job	*great strength and endurance *can fell two trees at one blow *can swing axe 16 hours without stopping *created the Great Lakes with my footprints *5 years experience
Special Requirements	I need to eat 20,000 calories a day.
Preferred Working Conditions and Why	I prefer to work with my great blue ox, Babe. The spread of his horns is the length of 42 axe handles. He can haul great quantities of wood.

Read the information on the table and use it to follow the directions below.

1. Write a key idea you learned about Paul.

   _____

   _____

   What details support that idea?

   _____

   _____

2. Write a key idea you learned about Babe.

   _____

   _____

   What details support that idea?

   _____

   _____

3. Write a brief summary of the information on the table.

   _____

   _____

   _____

Name

EXPLORE MYSTERIOUS ATLANTIS

ADVENTURE #26 Climb aboard a submarine to search the oceans for the lost city of Atlantis. People wonder if Atlantis really existed. You can help to solve the mystery once and for all!

1.

Atlantis was a large mythical island in the Atlantic Ocean. Plato, a writer in ancient Greece, wrote a tale about this island. The tale told of a great empire that existed on Atlantis. In the tale, earthquakes, floods, and great storms shook the whole island. During the great storms, the island sank into the sea.

Circle a key idea in the paragraph.
Write a brief summary of the information.

_____

_____

_____

_____

2.

For centuries, people were fascinated with Plato's tales about the island of Atlantis. Many wondered where it was and how it sank. Many wondered if it was a real place or just another Greek myth. Perhaps it really existed at one time. Over the years, many stories and fantasies have been told about a great city that lies beneath the ocean. Some think that it is still inhabited by sea creatures such as mermaids and mermen. Some scientists think the tales were inspired by a real island, the island of Thera in the Aegean Sea. This island was destroyed by a volcanic eruption around 1470 B.C.

Circle a key idea in the paragraph.
Write a brief summary of the information.

_____

_____

_____

_____

3.

The great mythical empire of Atlantis was built on an island in the Atlantic Ocean. Atlantis had powerful armies which planned to conquer all of the lands in the Mediterranean area. They had success in parts of Europe and North Africa, but the armies of Athens defeated them and drove them away.

Circle a key idea in the paragraph. Write a brief summary of the information.

_____

_____

_____

_____

Name _____

Common Core Reinforcement Activities: 5th Grade Language

SNOOP AROUND THE OCEAN

ADVENTURE #27 Help Dr. Deape as she snoops around in the ocean. Show that you know something about the stuff beneath the surface!

For each thing the two of you discover or bump into write a word (or two) to tell what you have found. Choose from the words below.

1. You both feel a movement where the water is rising and falling. _____

2. You get pushed up on the very top of a wave. _____

3. You dip down to the lowest point of a wave. _____

4. You get caught in the movement of more dense seawater as it goes toward less dense seawater. _____

5. You have a slight crack in your mask, and a tiny bit of seawater leaks into your mouth. It does not taste fresh! What causes that taste? _____

6. Your boat gets slowly washed toward shore with shallow water waves caused by the pull of gravity. _____

7. Dr. Deape tells you that these waves are caused by the gravitational pull three space bodies exert on each other. _____

8. You try to see the steeply dropping outer edge of the continental shelf, but do not get a good look at it. _____

9. The ocean is too murky to see any of the animals that live along the ocean bottom. _____

10. You do see plenty of tiny plants and animals that drift along the ocean surface. _____

BENTHOS   CONTINENTAL SHELF   TROUGH

WAVES   PLANKTON   CONTINENTAL SLOPE

PLAIN   CREST   EARTH

TIDES   SUN   MOON

EVAPORATES   COOLER   CURRENT

NUTRIENTS   RIFT ZONES

DISSOLVED SALTS   WARMER

Name _____

EAVESDROP ON HISTORY

ADVENTURE #28 Stumble into the 1787 Constitutional Convention in Philadelphia, Pennsylvania. Tiptoe through the sawdust on the pavement outside the Senate building that cuts down noise of the traffic. (These delegates do not want to be disturbed as they work on this document!) Sneak past the guards into the secret meetings.

Use what you learn to solve this puzzle about the *United States Constitution*.

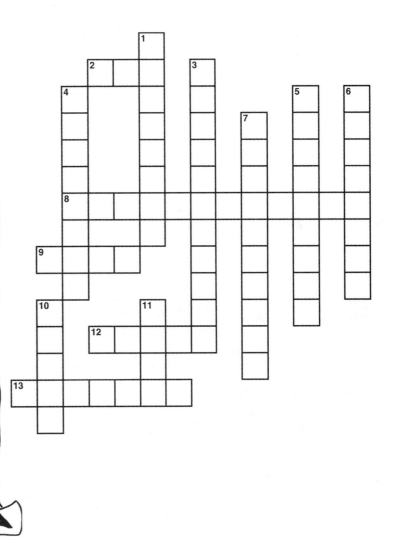

Across

2. number of senators from each state
8. the highest law of the U.S.
9. Congress makes the _____
12. to change the Constitution
13. serves a 6-year term

Down

1. made up of the Senate plus the House of Representatives
3. only colony that did not take part in the Constitutional Convention
4. branch of government that has courts
5. Chief Executive Officer of the U.S.
6. the U.S. government is a system of checks and _____
7. number of representatives from each state depends on the state's _____
10. number of branches of U.S. government
11. president's refusal to approve a law

Name _____

HEAD TO THE SPACE STATION

ADVENTURE #29 Fly on a rocket through space to visit the International Space Station (ISS). United States astronaut Shannon Lucid spent a record 188 days there. We won't keep you that long!

Read the information in the flier, and notice the structure of the text. Compare this to the text on the next page, page 57.

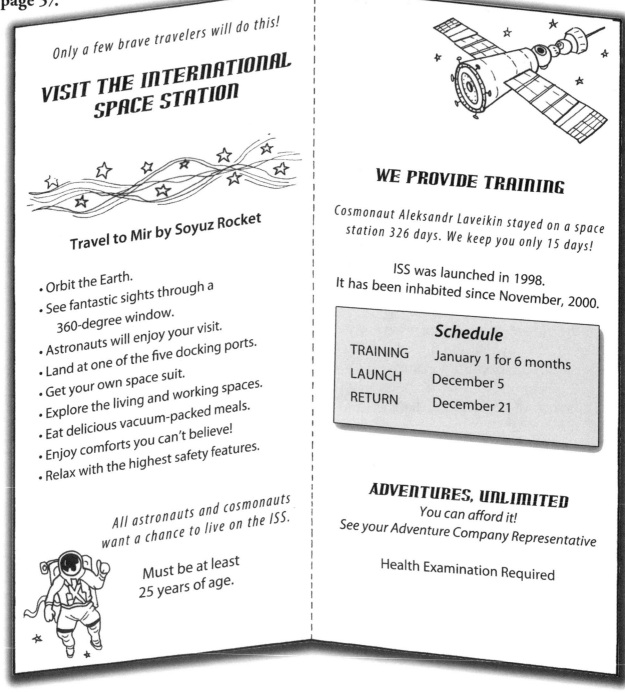

Only a few brave travelers will do this!

VISIT THE INTERNATIONAL SPACE STATION

Travel to Mir by Soyuz Rocket

- Orbit the Earth.
- See fantastic sights through a 360-degree window.
- Astronauts will enjoy your visit.
- Land at one of the five docking ports.
- Get your own space suit.
- Explore the living and working spaces.
- Eat delicious vacuum-packed meals.
- Enjoy comforts you can't believe!
- Relax with the highest safety features.

All astronauts and cosmonauts want a chance to live on the ISS.

Must be at least 25 years of age.

WE PROVIDE TRAINING

Cosmonaut Aleksandr Laveikin stayed on a space station 326 days. We keep you only 15 days!

ISS was launched in 1998.
It has been inhabited since November, 2000.

Schedule

TRAINING	January 1 for 6 months
LAUNCH	December 5
RETURN	December 21

ADVENTURES, UNLIMITED
You can afford it!
See your Adventure Company Representative

Health Examination Required

Use with page 57.

Name

56

Read the information about International Space Station on this page and the previous page, page 56. Compare the two texts.

The International Space Station is an artificial satellite built and owned by a group of nations. As long as a football field, it has as much living space as a six-bedroom house and weighs almost a million pounds (454,000 kilograms). Its purpose is to be a laboratory, observatory, and factory in space.

Since its launch in 2000, over 200 people have lived on the space station. Astronauts see 16 sunsets and sunrises a day as the ISS orbits Earth every 90 minutes. Much of the time, they work—doing scientific experiments and maintaining the station. They rest, exercise, and eat a carefully planned diet. There is not enough water for showers—so they have to keep clean with water jets and wet wipes. They are weightless, so when they eat, the food has to be secured to keep it from floating off. When they sleep, they stay attached to a wall.

Needless to say, when the space travelers get back to Earth, it takes a few days to get used to living with gravity again! Even with all the inconveniences, astronauts love their experience. And plenty of others want the space experience too! Right now, for private citizens, it costs about $20 million for 6 months of training and travel on a *Soyuz* rocket to stay 10 days on the ISS.

1. What is similar about the two texts? _____

_____

_____

2. How does the structure of the two texts differ? _____

_____

_____

3. How does the content of the two texts differ? _____

_____

_____

4. How does the structure of the text affect the message or purpose? _____

_____

_____

Use with page 56.

Name _____

CRACK THE CASES!

ADVENTURE #30 Be a detective for a day. Try to crack some unsolved mystery cases!

In each of these mysteries, a narrator describes the events and clues. On the next page, a witness to each event tells the story. Read both versions. Compare the two.

The Case of the Missing Pizzas

At noon it was discovered.
Thirteen pizzas were missing from Papa Gino's.
Size 10 footprints were found at the scene.
Three suspects were caught.
Bart had pizza sauce on his shirt.
Burt had cheese shreds in his hair.
Brett had a guilty smirk on his face.
Burt wears size 12 shoes.
Bart slept until noon.
Brett wears size 8 shoes.
Police solved the mystery.
They arrested one of the suspects.
Who stole the pizzas?

The Great Escape

The room has one door.
The door is locked.
It cannot be unlocked from inside.
The room has no windows.
The room has a cracked skylight.
There is a ladder in the room.
The man in the room has no tools.
At midnight it was raining.
By 2:00 P.M., the temperature was below freezing.
The cat slept on the outside step.
The cat has not been disturbed.
The man is not in the room.
How did he escape?

A Crash in the Night

The night is dark.
Long shadows lurk in every corner.
The streets are empty.
Only a lone streetlight lights a corner.
Heavy mist hangs in the air.
There is not a sound.
Nothing is moving.
Suddenly, a crash splits the silence.
Shattered glass sprinkles to the ground.
Then it is quiet again.
What caused the crash?

Use with page 59.

Name

Compare the witness reports to the narrators' reports on page 58. For each event, list differences between the two accounts. Use a separate piece of paper.

Then, solve at least one of the mysteries. Tell some classmates your solution and how you cracked the case.

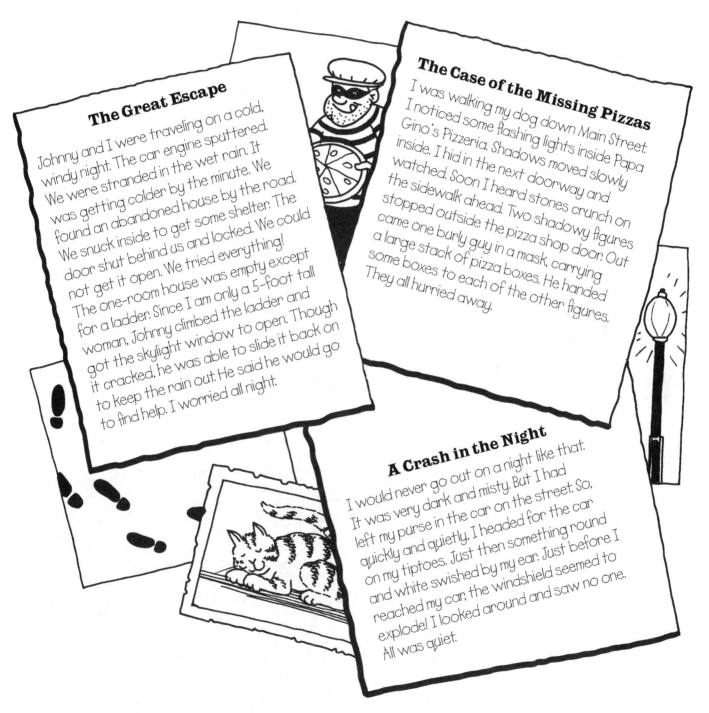

The Great Escape

Johnny and I were traveling on a cold, windy night. The car engine sputtered. We were stranded in the wet rain. It was getting colder by the minute. We found an abandoned house by the road. We snuck inside to get some shelter. The door shut behind us and locked. We could not get it open. We tried everything! The one-room house was empty except for a ladder. Since I am only a 5-foot tall woman, Johnny climbed the ladder and got the skylight window to open. Though it cracked, he was able to slide it back on to keep the rain out. He said he would go to find help. I worried all night.

The Case of the Missing Pizzas

I was walking my dog down Main Street. I noticed some flashing lights inside Papa Gino's Pizzeria. Shadows moved slowly inside. I hid in the next doorway and watched. Soon I heard stones crunch on the sidewalk ahead. Two shadowy figures stopped outside the pizza shop door. Out came one burly guy in a mask, carrying a large stack of pizza boxes. He handed some boxes to each of the other figures. They all hurried away.

A Crash in the Night

I would never go out on a night like that. It was very dark and misty. But I had left my purse in the car on the street. So, quickly and quietly, I headed for the car on my tiptoes. Just then something round and white swished by my ear. Just before I reached my car, the windshield seemed to explode! I looked around and saw no one. All was quiet.

TAKE A RIDE WITH "THE KING"

Most Expensive Items
of Rock Stars' Belongings Sold at Auctions

Item	Year of Sale	Price
John Lennon's 1965 Rolls-Royce Phantom V touring limousine	1985	$ 2,299,000
Jimi Hendrix's Fender Stratocaster electric guitar	2008	$ 490,000
An acoustic guitar that had been owned by George Michael, Paul McCartney, and David Bowie	1994	$ 341,000
Buddy Holly's Gibson electric guitar	1990	$ 242,000
John Lennon's 1970 Mercedes-Benz 600 limousine	1989	$ 213,125
Elvis Presley's 1942 Martin D-18 guitar	1995	$ 180,000
Elvis Presley's 1963 Rolls-Royce Phantom V touring limousine	1986	$ 162,800
Charlie Parker's Grafton saxophone	1994	$ 144,925
John Lennon's recording of his singing at a 1957 church fair	1994	$ 121,675
Buddy Holly's Fender Stratocaster electric guitar	1990	$ 110,000

ADVENTURE #31
This one will take a bit of time travel. We'll take you back to the 1960s for a ride in Elvis's Rolls Royce. A lot of his fans will be jealous of you!

1. Which listed items are not musical instruments? _____

_____

2. How would you compare the cost of John Lennon's recording with the cost of his Mercedes-Benz limousine? _____

_____

3. How would you compare the cost of John Lennon's 1965 limousine with Elvis's limousine? _____

_____

4. What are the benefits of this text structure in presenting information? _____

_____

_____

Name _____

FOLLOW A CRIME-LINE

ADVENTURE #32 Spend some time with the great crime professor, Dr. Iam Shrewd. Learn how to make a crime-line timeline to help solve the stickiest crimes.

Professor Shrewd investigated the disappearance of a rare book from Ms. Rathskeller's shop, *Blue Dragon Used Books*. He created this timeline to record information he found. Use the timeline to answer the questions.

Listen up, Detectives-in-Training! Take notes at the crime scene and make a timeline.

TIMELINE

7:59 a.m. Ms. Rathskeller puts an *Open* sign in the window of her store.

8:01 a.m. She unlocks the door.

8:04 a.m. She goes to fix her morning cup of jasmine tea in the back room.

8:10 a.m. Mr. Fiddle, the first visitor of the day, comes in to pick up a book he had ordered.

8:15 a.m. Ms. Rathskeller unlocks the rare book display case to tidy it.

8:20 a.m. Mr. Fiddle leaves to catch his bus.

8:21 a.m. Ms. Rathskeller gets her first phone call of the day from the bank.

8:25 a.m. The second visitor of the day (an unknown person) comes in to ask directions to the post office, and leaves.

8:30 a.m. Ms. Rathskeller goes into the back room to rinse out her teacup. She hears the bell jingle on the door.

8:32 a.m. She comes out to see the third visitor of the day, who purchases an inexpensive paperback.

8:35 a.m. She receives her second phone call, requesting information on a book. She has to go and look it up in the card catalog.

8:38 a.m. The third visitor leaves.

8:42 a.m. She discovers the rare book is missing from the unlocked case and calls the police.

1. What time was the first phone call of the day? _____

2. How long did the first visitor stay in the store? _____

3. How long was the second visitor in the store? _____

4. How long did the third visitor stay in the store? _____

5. What time did Mr. Fiddle arrive at the shop? _____

6. The rare bookcase was opened at what time? _____

7. What time does she discover the rare book missing? _____

8. Does the third visitor leave before or after the second phone call? _____

9. When did Ms. Rathskeller unlock the door? _____

10. How long was Mr. Fiddle in the shop before the case was opened? _____

11. Who do you think stole the rare book, and why do you think so? _____

_____

Name

BE A HUMAN SPIDER

ADVENTURE #33 You've watched Spiderman and real-life characters do it. Now try it yourself! Climb some of the world's tallest buildings. Be a daredevil and scale skyscrapers in the tradition of Alain Robert, "the French Spider-Man."

Use the information on the graph to answer the questions.

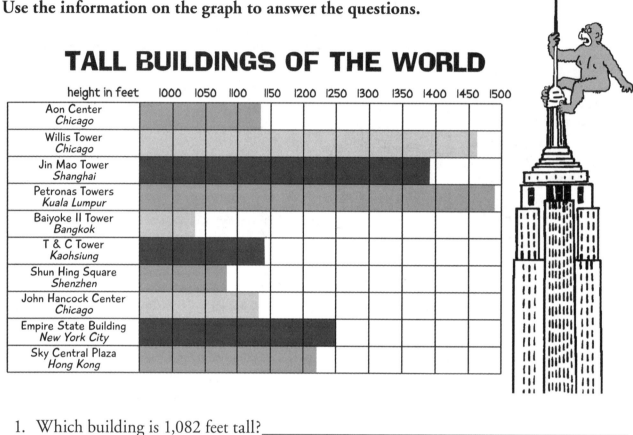

TALL BUILDINGS OF THE WORLD

1. Which building is 1,082 feet tall?_____

2. Which is the tallest building shown? _____

3. Which is the shortest building shown? _____

4. Which two buildings are closest in height?_____

5. Which building is 1,250 feet tall?_____

6. Which building is 1,381 feet tall?_____

7. Which building is 1,127 feet tall?_____

8. Which building is about 50 feet higher than the Sky Central Plaza? _____

9. Which building is about 100 feet shorter than the T & C Tower? _____

10. Which building is about 30 feet taller than the Willis Tower? _____

Name _____

DROP INTO THE ALPS

ADVENTURE #34 There's nothing quite like a helicopter adventure! Bring your skis, and we'll supply the rest. We will drop you into the Swiss Alps for the most extraordinary ski experience of your life!

Swiss SkiDrop, Inc.
HELICOPTER SCHEDULE

DEPARTURE CITY	Destination	Departure Days	Return Days
ZURICH	Drop 1	Tues, Thurs	Fri, Sun
	Drop 2	Wed, Sat	Mon, Thurs
	Drop 3	Sun, Wed	Tues, Fri
BASEL	Drop 1	Wed, Sat	Sun, Wed
	Drop 2	Sun, Wed	Tues, Fri
	Drop 3	Thurs, Sun	Sat, Tues
BERN	Drop 1	Fri, Tues	Mon, Fri
	Drop 2	Wed, Tues	Sun, Fri
	Drop 3	Sat, Wed	Tues, Fri
LAUSANNE	Drop 1	Mon, Fri	Wed, Sun
	Drop 2	Thurs, Tues	Mon, Thurs
	Drop 3	Sun, Tues	Wed, Sat
CHUR	Drop 1	Thurs	Mon
	Drop 2	Mon	Fri

Use the information on the table to answer the questions.

1. Leaving from Basel, can you fly to Drop 1 and stay for only 3 days (including travel days)?_____

2. If you wanted to head for Drop 2 on a Wednesday, from what cities could you depart?
_____

3. Where can you go on Tuesday from Lausanne? _____

4. Can you fly to Drop 3 from Chur? _____

5. What days can you return to Bern from Drop 3? _____

6. Can you return to Zurich from Drop 2 on Tuesday? _____

7. If you want to leave Zurich on Wednesday and return the following Monday, which destination must you choose?_____

8. Can you return from Drop 1 to Chur on a Monday? _____

9. How many choices for departure are there on Friday?_____

10. How many choices for returns are there on Sunday?_____

Name _____

CHEER FOR THE SLUGS

ADVENTURE #35 It may be the only slug race in the world. Would you want to miss it? Travel into the giant redwoods of California for one of the most unusual races you'll ever see. You get front row seats. You can even race a slug if you want to!

Morning Edition

Daily News

Valley Weather: Partly Cloudy

Vol. XXXIX No 14235   Sunny Valley, California July 10, 2012   35¢

SLUG RACES COMING TO AREA SOON

There's more wildlife to watch and enjoy next month in the Pacific Coast redwoods of Northern California.

Visitors flock to Prairie Creek Redwoods State Park on the Pacific Ocean for many reasons. After they play in the ocean, they can watch elk, bears, bobcats, and foxes, which are plentiful in the ancient forest park. Campers can park trailers and hike the beautiful trails through the canyons to the ocean.

But next month, there will be another fascinating reason to visit the park. In August, the park will be the setting of the Annual Slug Derby. A variety of races will be held and prizes will be awarded to winning slugs in several categories.

One of last year's top winning banana slugs poses with her owner and her trophy. Over seven hundred spectators watched the races last year.

Two hundred trophies made by locals will be given. There will be food and fun for everyone.

Visitors are invited to attend the derby. "You can bring your own slug, or we'll loan you one from our slugarium at the visitors' center," says Park Ranger Robert Roberts. Park rangers have already started hunting for speedy slugs. Visitors need to know, however, that this is a very competitive race. Therefore, any slugs brought in from the outside will be given a slug drug test before they are eligible to take part in the races.

For information about the Banana Slug Derby, call the Prairie Creek Park Visitor's Center at 707-488-2171.

Answer the questions on this page and the next page (page 65).

1. How does the author tell you that there is wildlife to enjoy in the redwoods of Northern California?

   _____

   _____

2. How does the author tell the reader that the public is welcome at the slug races?

   _____

   _____

Use with page 65.

Name

Read the news article on page 64. Then answer the questions on page 64 and on this page.

3. Slugs brought in from the outside are tested, while other slugs are not. How does the writer explain this?

_____

_____

_____

_____

_____

_____

4. The author claims that "this is a very competitive race." How does the author support this idea?

_____

_____

_____

_____

_____

5. From the article, would you expect this event to be a short one or a long one? _____

How did the text help you with your answer?

_____

_____

_____

_____

_____

Use with page 64.

Name _____

VISIT CAMELOT

ADVENTURE #36 Meet King Arthur. Visit Camelot. Get your very own suit of armor. Learn to fight a dragon, if you wish. Many have dreamed of this adventure. You can actually live it!

Sir Prance-a-lot the knight fiercely battles a menacing, fire-breathing, winged dragon. How brave he is to step right up to the dragon—surrounded by the powerful tail and within reach of the terrible claws. The skilled warrior steps forward to plunge his lance into the dragon. This ends the reign of the creature that has terrorized villages and threatened the castle.

Meanwhile, the knight's mighty horse spies a damsel in distress. He does not wait for help from Sir Prance-a-lot. Instead, he uses his power and wit to unravel the tangled ropes. The damsel is ever grateful to the knight for the rescue.

Review the story and the illustration to answer the questions.

1. The writer calls the knight "brave." How does he support this claim?_____
   _____
   _____

2. The dragon is described as "menacing." What evidence does the writer give to support this?
   _____
   _____

3. The story says the damsel is grateful to the prince for rescuing her.
   How well does the writer support this idea with the text or illustration?_____
   _____
   _____
   _____

Name _____

SEARCH FOR NESSIE

ADVENTURE #37 Join the hunt for the Loch Ness Monster. Start your search at the library where investigative reporter Bea Sharp will help you find an encyclopedia entry and a poem about this creature.

Loch Ness Monster

is a large animal that some people believe lives in Loch Ness, a large lake in Northern Scotland. There are hundreds of reported sightings. But if it does exist, it is hard to prove.

The creature is nicknamed Nessie. It is described as having a long, slim neck, flippers, and one or two humps. Some believe it may be related to a dinosaur-like reptile or a present-day sea animal like the seal or manatee.

Sightings have been reported as far back as A.D. 565. In 1930, when a new highway made the lake more accessible, the sightings increased. People search the lake in boats or with diving equipment. In 1934, a doctor took a photo that shows a long, dinosaur-like neck and a head extending out of the water.

Since 1960, scientists have used sonar to explore Loch Ness. They have found large moving bodies in the lake, but do not agree on whether the sonar detected one big creature or a school of fish.

In 1972 and 1975, researchers from the Academy of Applied Science in Boston took underwater photos of what they claimed was the Loch Ness Monster. However, many experts question the value of these photos.

Whether or not Nessie is really there, she attracts thousands of tourists and searchers to Loch Ness each year. She also inspires the imagination of many children, adults, artists, and writers.

Terror in Scotland

I've seen the fierce winged dragon
With mouth of flame and smoke
And dreamed of the elusive Sasquatch—
Still chasing me when I awoke.

I've ridden the great Greek Satyr
With body part man, part beast.
I've battled the monstrous Hydra
Who wore nine heads, at least!

I've flown on the grotesque Griffin—
Eagle head, lion body and tail.
I've come to face the Yeti,
And shuddered till I grew pale.

I've danced with a mighty Unicorn
(Now doesn't that sound absurd?)
I've escaped a deadly Siren—
A creature half woman, half bird.

But I've never shrieked in horror,
Never trembled and shook with dread.
I have never cried like a baby,
Nor stopped breathing like the dead.
No, I never knew sheer terror,
Not awake or asleep, I confess,
Until I saw, for a moment
The Monster of Loch Ness—
The massive
Rising
Grasping
Writhing
SERPENT
Of
Loch
Ness.

After you read the above information, follow the instructions on the next page, page 68.

Use with page 68.

Name

What have you learned about the Loch Ness Monster from the two texts on page 67 (and the illustration on this page)?

Use this space to make a list of what you have learned. Be ready to use your list to share information about this topic in an essay, news item, or speech.

_____

_____

_____

_____

_____

_____

_____

_____

_____

_____

_____

_____

_____

_____

_____

_____

_____

_____

_____

_____

Use with page 67.

Name

READING

FOUNDATIONAL SKILLS

Grade 5

BEACH MISBEHAVIOR

There's a bit of misbehavior at the beach today! What does *misbehavior* mean? The prefix *mis* changes the word *behavior* to a word that means "bad behavior."

A **prefix** changes the meaning of the root word in some way. Look at the meanings of the prefixes on the chart. Use these to write the meaning of each word below.

Meanings of Some Prefixes

a	(on)
anti	(against)
be	(make)
dis, im, un	(not)
inter	(between)
mid	(middle)
mini	(small)
mis	(bad, wrong)
multi	(many)
over	(too much)
pre	(before)
re	(again)
sub	(under, below)
trans	(across)
uni	(one)

Read each word and write its meaning.

1. uniform _____

2. ashore _____

3. belittle _____

4. substandard _____

5. misread _____

6. overstate _____

7. midstream _____

8. anticrime _____

9. transoceanic _____

10. afoot _____

11. revisit _____

12. preseason _____

13. multitalented _____

14. immovable _____

15. miniskirt _____

16. international _____

17. unspoiled _____

18. displeased _____

Name

Suffix	Meaning
en	(to make)
ful	(full of, like)
fy	(to cause to be)
ic	(like, pertaining to)
ism	(act or quality of)
less	(without)
lets	(small)
ment	(act or quality of)
ness	(state or condition of)
or	(one who)
ous	(full of, like)
ship	(state or quality of)
some	(full of)
ward	(toward)
y	(like, full of)

DANGER AT SEA

A **suffix** is a word part that can be added to the end of a word to change the word's meaning.

What will happen to the storm-tossed ship? These words will give you some clues to help you imagine what will happen.

Read each word. Choose at least ten. Write the meanings below the words.

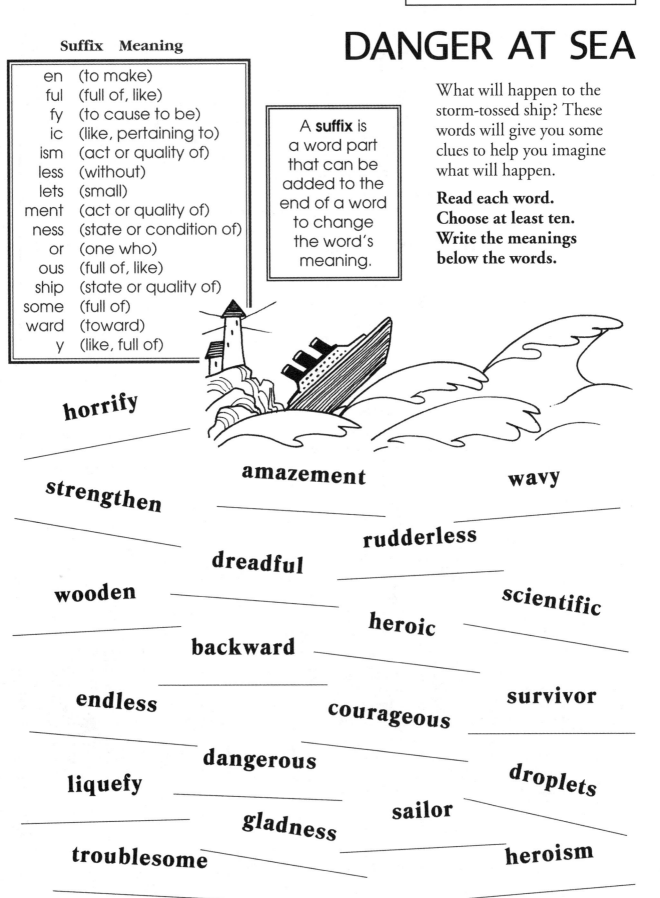

horrify

amazement

wavy

strengthen

rudderless

dreadful

wooden

scientific

heroic

backward

endless

courageous

survivor

dangerous

liquefy

droplets

gladness

sailor

troublesome

heroism

Name

Common Core Reinforcement Activities: 5th Grade Language

UNFORGETTABLE!

When you come face-to-face with a weird sea creature, it is a truly unforgettable experience! The word *unforgettable* is built from the root word *forget*. Then other word parts (a prefix and a suffix) are added to the word. If you know your roots, you can read and create all kinds of words.

Choose the right root from the box to form each of the words described.

Root	Meaning
act	(act, do)
aqua	(water)
cap	(head)
don	(give)
dynam	(energy)
frac	(break)
geo	(earth)
graph	(write)
gyr	(whirl)
ject	(throw)
ign	(light)
mob	(move)
oper	(work)
therm	(heat)
view	(see)

1. _____ometer   *instrument to measure heat*

2. _____logy   *study of earth*

3. co_____ate   *work together*

4. pro _____ ile   *something thrown*

5. _____tain   *head of a team*

6. _____ ion   *number broken in parts*

7. re _____   *see again*

8. im _____ ile   *unmovable*

9. _____ ition   *act of lighting*

10. auto _____   *write on your own*

11. _____ ation   *act of whirling*

12. _____ ation   *something given*

13. _____ tic   *pertaining to water*

14. _____ture   *something broken*

15. _____ or   *one who acts*

16. _____ic   *pertaining to energy*

uh oh!

Name

BELOW THE SEA

Root   Meaning

Root	Meaning
ann	(year)
aqua	(water)
ast	(star)
auto	(self)
bene	(good, well)
bio	(life)
cycl	(circle)
frag	(break)
geo	(earth)
graph	(write)
grav	(heavy)
labor	(work)
lib	(book)
loc	(place)
mar	(sea)
meter	(measure)
mini	(small)
mot, mov	(move)
ped	(foot)
pend	(hang)
port	(carry)
sol	(sun)
vac	(empty)
term	(end)

A submarine travels far down under the surface of the ocean. *Submarine* is a word formed from the root word *mar* (meaning "sea") and the prefix *sub* (meaning "below") and the suffix *ine* (meaning "relating to").

Read the roots and their meanings. Add a suffix or prefix (or both) to form 20 new words. Try to make at least 20 words!

_____   _____

_____   _____

_____   _____

_____   _____

_____   _____

_____   _____

_____   _____

_____   _____

_____   _____

_____   _____

Name _____

Common Core Reinforcement Activities: 5th Grade Language

AN UNUSUAL DISCOVERY

It's not unusual for a diver to find the wreck of a ship. What is strange is to discover a ship full of words! Interestingly, every one of these words could be part of a compound word like the word *shipwreck*!

Use a word on the boat as part of a compound word. Form as many compound words as you can. Make a compound by adding another word that is not on the ship to the beginning or end of one of these. Or combine two of these together. Write the words you create in the blank space. Use the back of the paper for more.

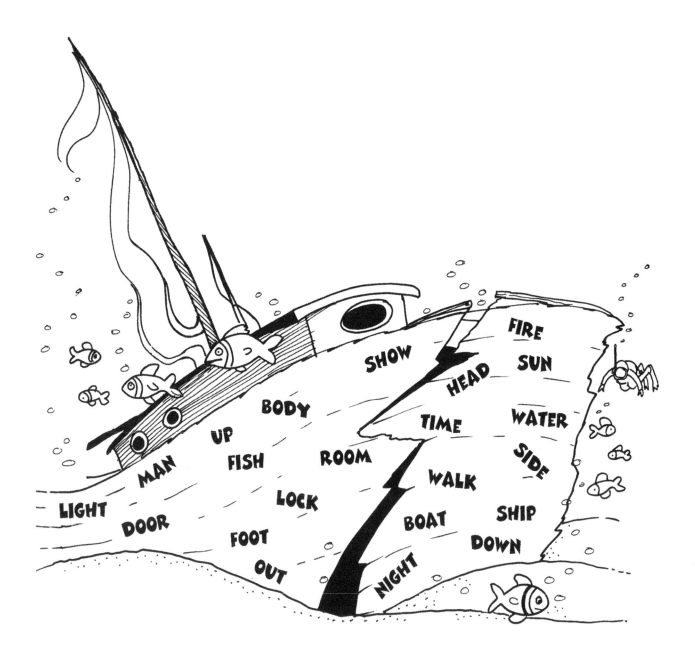

Name

A BRAKE IN THE PEER

What's wrong with this title? It's a case of mixed-up homophones! What should it be?

Read about all the happenings on the beach today. Circle the correct word or words for each sentence.

1. Something caused a major (break, brake) in the (pier, peer)!

2. They'll have to (billed, build) a new (peer, pier).

3. Three kids (berried, buried) their dad in the sand.

4. Lots of swimmers enjoyed the (serf, surf).

5. A (loan, lone) shark swam along the (beech, beach).

6. Everyone ran from a monstrous (wave, waive).

7. Sanya's (cash, cache) of shells was washed away.

8. Catching that wave was a huge (feat, feet) for the surfers.

9. Don't get carried away by the strong (currant, current)!

10. Did you catch a glimpse of any (crews, cruise) ships?

11. We watched (crews, cruise) sweep along in sleek (skulls, sculls).

12. One of the paddlers lost an (ore, or, oar).

13. Sailors tied (taut, taught) lines to the dock.

14. At exactly 4 p.m., a (dense, dents) fog rolled onto the beach.

Name

Common Core Reinforcement Activities: 5th Grade Language

WHAT YOU SEE IN THE SEA

What Ramona sees in the sea is a lot of fish with words! Curiously, both words on each fish sound the same.

Choose a pair of words to complete each sentence below. Be sure you write the correct word in the correct spot in the sentence.

1. I did _____ right past that sea lion. She must have _____ a ton!

2. I intended to _____ my flippers. Now _____ did I leave them?

3. We _____ the jet ski for an hour, then _____ our boat to shore.

4. Did you _____ that a pirate landed right _____?

5. He looked me in the _____ and said, "_____, _____, Matey!"

6. Then I saw a wet dog _____ at the shoreline to wash his _____.

7. Next, I watched as a bumpy _____ _____ his bullfrog friend to shore.

8. I wonder _____ this perfect _____ will hold.

9. What's that noise? Is it the _____ of a beached _____?

10. Have you ever _____ such a spectacular underwater _____?

Name _____

WHERE WOULD YOU FIND THIS?

Fisherman Fred has found some very strange things in his net. Is that where they belong?

Decide where each one of these things would be found. Circle the correct choice.

Where would you find . . .

1. . . . a **grotto**?
   a. in a stomach
   b. on the edge of a sea
   c. underneath a dog's fur

2. . . . a **horde**?
   a. at a parade
   b. on a banana split
   c. in a flowerpot

3. . . . a **gourmand**?
   a. at a banquet
   b. woven into a carpet
   c. on a sheet of music

4. . . . a **kiosk**?
   a. on top of a steeple
   b. in toothpaste
   c. in a mall

5. . . . a **sieve**?
   a. in a sleeve
   b. in a kitchen drawer
   c. on an easel

6. . . . a **gutter**?
   a. in a sundae
   b. along a roof
   c. under your tongue

7. . . . a **soufflé**?
   a. on a trombone
   b. on a menu
   c. under a beach towel

8. . . . a **femur**?
   a. inside a tooth
   b. on a lobster
   c. under your skin

9. . . . some **plankton**?
   a. on a salad
   b. in a puppet show
   c. near the ocean surface

10. . . . a **jester**?
    a. in a silly play
    b. in a car engine
    c. inside a glove

11. . . . a **wraith**?
    a. in a ghost story
    b. in a bathtub
    c. on a dinner plate

12. . . . a **scalpel**?
    a. in a doctor's office
    b. riding a ski lift
    c. under a wig

13. . . . a **tentacle**?
    a. in a tent
    b. on an octopus
    c. riding a pony

Name _____

Common Core Reinforcement Activities: 5th Grade Language

WHERE WOULD YOU FIND THAT?

Fisherwoman Freeda has found some more weird stuff in her net. Is this where it belongs?

Decide where each of these would be found. Circle the correct choice or choices.

Where would you find . . .

1. . . . an **orca**?
   a. at a computer
   b. in a church
   c. swimming in the ocean

2. . . . a **collage**?
   a. driving a car
   b. singing in a choir
   c. in an art gallery

3. . . . an **avalanche**?
   a. on a snowy mountain
   b. in a pickup truck
   c. heading for the moon

4. . . . a **tango**?
   a. at a candy store
   b. at a dance contest
   c. at a hairshop

5. . . . a **pancreas**?
   a. in a shell
   b. near your spine
   c. in a dresser drawer

6. . . . a **garnish**?
   a. on a sandwich
   b. beneath your toenail
   c. acting on a stage

7. . . . a **sequin**?
   a. in a movie rental store
   b. in a cookie
   c. on a prom dress

8. . . . a **plot**?
   a. in a story
   b. in a geometry problem
   c. on a snowplow

9. . . . a **bassoon**?
   a. swimming in a pond
   b. in a flower pot
   c. in an orchestra

10. . . . a **tourniquet**?
    a. on a tennis court
    b. in a first aid kit
    c. in a wedding

11. . . . an **anecdote**?
    a. in a book
    b. inside a camera
    c. around a doctor's neck

12. . . . a **stanza**?
    a. in a fishing net
    b. in a poem
    c. in a lake

13. . . . an **archipelago**?
    a. on a quilt
    b. in a cathedral ceiling
    c. in an ocean

Name

WRITING

Grade 5

Aunt Lucinda's Advice
Don't ever...
talk back to your mother
save an ice cream bar in your pocket
forget to pay your taxes
go into a burning building
try to interview the gorilla at the zoo
wear your pajamas to work
stand on top of a bridge in the wind
eat a sandwich without mayonnaise
swallow peach pits

IN MY OPINION

A letter to the editor of a newspaper or magazine is a good way to express an opinion. Readers comment on something that has been published in the magazine or newspaper, or they just express an opinion about any public matter.

Express your opinion in a letter to the editor. Follow the instructions on the next page (page 81).

Dear Editor:

Your coverage of school issues and events in this town is horrible. I am surprised and annoyed at the shallow *City News* coverage.

In the past year, ninety percent of your articles about school have been reports of sporting events. You have ignored the other wonderful accomplishments and events of our schools. It is as if academics, music, drama, and many arts events do not exist. Only 18% of the town's public school students participate in sports. You are giving no attention to the activities of the other 81%.

Not only do you over-report on sports, you ignore most of the sports. Most stories feature the same students again and again in the flashiest sports of basketball and football. Students in Mansfield participate in twelve other sports. Furthermore, your coverage is mainly about boys' teams. Girls get little attention.

You are depriving your readers of a full view of student activities. Readers would have a more truthful and admiring view of the schools and their students if you would examine this paper's biases and do a better job with your reporting about the whole picture of education.

Sincerely.
Tomas Bassen, Grade 8

Dear Editor;

The noise in our city is getting out of hand. Music from local clubs, people shouting speeches in the park, and all kinds of noisy vehicles are spoiling our pleasant town,

My friends and I keep a journal of the times and places we are disturbed by noise coming from public areas. We have many examples from all times of the year, in all kinds of weather, and in many parts of the town. The noise affects us in our homes and outside our homes in places we go for recreation and entertainment,

I urge the town council to discuss the request we sent them to do something about the noise!

Sincerely,
Jojo James

Dear Editor:

Whatever happened to books? Not enough people hold that wonderful square thing in their hands, turn the pages, underline and write comments, and enjoy the pleasures of a real book!

Kids my age live on smartphones, notebooks, and tablets. We read everything from Tweets to whole books and magazines. But there is something so satisfying about a book.

Let's have all ages of people in our community get together and sell, buy, loan, share, and read books!

Lucy LeGrande

Use with page 81.

Name

Write a letter to the editor that gives your opinion. Use one of the ideas below, or write about any other idea.

Introduce the topic. Give your opinion. Give reasons for your opinion.
Write a clear ending.

Dear Editor:

school lunches

wasted resources

grades

a
particular
rule

school dress codes

value of
grammar

food quality
in local restaurants

school schedule

SOMETHING
HAPPENING
IN YOUR COUNTRY

SOMETHING
HAPPENING
IN YOUR TOWN

kids having cell phones

kids on the
Internet

things that should change   kids and video games   books kids should read

Use with page 80.

Name _____

CONVINCE ME!

A jingle is a catchy advertising slogan or ad—often set to music or rhythm. Its purpose is to convince buyers to try a product. Murphy wrote a jingle in the form of a rap for a flavored dental floss. Since the ad ran on TV, sales of the floss have tripled!

Read Murphy's rap-jingle below. Then create a short jingle (in any form) for each of the products on the right. Name your product. Then write the jingle here or on the back of the paper.

You use that sonic thing to brush
   with the buzzing sound
You swig a rinse and gargle juice
   where germ killers abound
You buy that whitenin' stuff so that
   your chops are lookin' bright.
But you will have no healthy teeth:
   you're just not doin' it right.

You hear me now? Well, listen up.
   You're not doin' tooth care right.
You gotta floss. You gotta floss—
   morning, noon, and night.
Get MEGA-FLOSS, the super floss
   that scrapes out all the goo.
Back and forth, three times a day.
   It's what you gotta do.

Try the spicy pizza kind.
   Try many more that please.
Trust me here, you'll fight them off—
   those nasty cavities.
Buy this floss. Buy a lot!
   It's what I'm tellin' you.
You'll love the taste. You'll get results.
   It's what you've gotta do.

motor oil-flavored toothpaste

DVD of pig-calling lessons

frozen rattlesnake steaks

Name

TERRIBLE CHOICES

Barrel-riding over Niagara Falls is not a good choice for an afternoon adventure.

There are great places to take a vacation, and there are some not-so-great places! Of course, people have different opinions about this.

Choose a place that you think would be a terrible choice for a vacation. It can be real or fictitious.

Give the name of the place. Tell what to bring and how to survive while there. Make sure your writing has a beginning, middle, and end.

Name

GREAT FOOD—YOUR WAY

Everybody has a favorite food or drink. Here's a chance for you to share something you love and know how to make!

Choose a food, drink, or snack that takes some doing to prepare (not something out of a package). List the ingredients and equipment. Then write step-by-step instructions that describe exactly how to make it so it turns out right. At the end, make any comment you want that gives more information about this marvelous creation.

Recipe for

_____

Name

ROCK IN THE FUTURE

You know how exciting it is to watch a live, televised, or video performance by your favorite musical performers. Just imagine what such concerts will be like in the future!

Write a brief story about a performance in the Cosmic Arena in the year 3500. Capture the reader with your beginning. Write an exciting plot with good details to support the ideas. Add a satisfying conclusion.

Name _____

85

Common Core Reinforcement Activities: 5th Grade Language

CLIFFHANGERS

Everybody loves a cliffhanger! It's a tale that leads you to an exciting, breathtaking, mysterious, or dangerous point. Then, it leaves you hanging! You don't know what happens next. Read Charlie's cliffhanger. Notice how he leaves you wondering what will happen next.

Joe knew it was not a good idea to be in the school at night. If it weren't for that math test the next day, he would never have gone there. He just had to have the math book he had left in his locker. Otherwise, he would fail the test. He had hoped to find a janitor working at the school, but there was no one there. Surprisingly, the door from the parking lot was unlocked. "I'll just run in, grab my book, and race right back out!" he told his mom. He flipped on the hall light and hurried to his locker. His hands shook as he tried the combination. He had to do it twice. Just as he got the math book and slammed his locker shut, the light went out. He heard no sounds. Everything was black! Quickly, he headed back down the hall to the door and pushed against it. To his shock, the door was locked. He could not get out! "It's a good thing Mom is waiting just outside the door in the car!" he said to himself. "She'll see me and get help." When he looked out the window, the parking lot was empty!

Finish the cliffhanger. Give it an interesting, satisfying ending. Then go on to page 87. Ponder the cliffhanger ideas, and write your own!

_____

_____

_____

_____

_____

_____

_____

Use with page 87.

Name

Write the beginning and middle of your own cliffhanger. (Use an idea from this page or one of your own.) Include something surprising or mysterious to catch the interest of your readers and inspire their imagination. Then, trade cliffhangers with a classmate. Finish each other's tales.

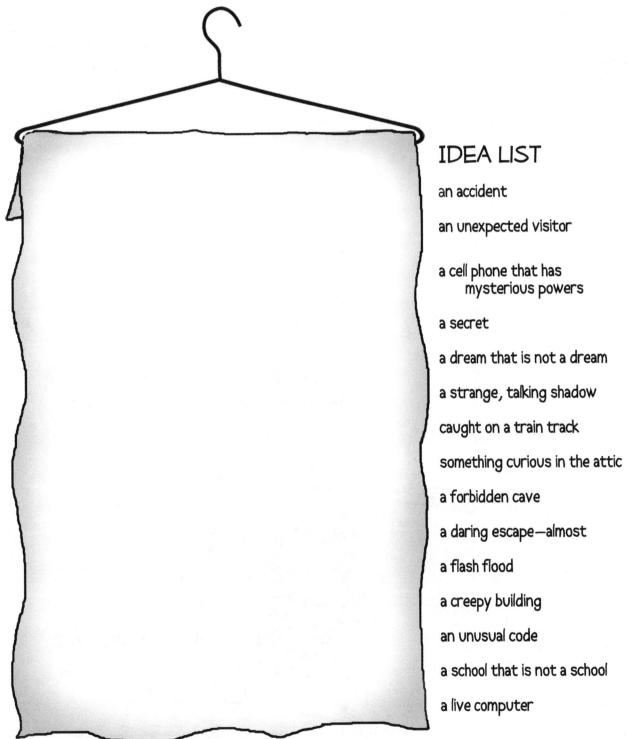

IDEA LIST

an accident

an unexpected visitor

a cell phone that has
    mysterious powers

a secret

a dream that is not a dream

a strange, talking shadow

caught on a train track

something curious in the attic

a forbidden cave

a daring escape—almost

a flash flood

a creepy building

an unusual code

a school that is not a school

a live computer

Use with page 86.

Name

Common Core Reinforcement Activities: 5th Grade Language

WORDS ON THE MOVE

The words just don't seem to want to sit still on the page today! They keep slipping and sliding all over. Murphy, the magazine editor, is preparing a page with writing that looks as if it were painted on the page instead of written in nice, neat lines. You could call this painted writing!

Read the page. Then choose one of the ideas from the Idea File, and try some painted writing of your own on another piece of paper.

SPARK magazine —— PAINTED POEMS

COFFEE

Warm and steamy, I brew down
And swim around. I jump down,
I jump down into a big cozy mug.
I stir around with some sweet tasty
Cream. Once I settle down a little, I enjoy
Myself and start to doze, until my warm
And sweet, sweet life is stirred and
Mixed and swallowed down. Coffee.
I'm new again in rich dark
Beans. I grind and grind
And brew and stir.*

Soft dough swirls with plump raisins, and sugary cinnamon buttery icing.

A slithery, slinky snake sneaks under my desk, so silently and stealthily, like a whisper across my feet.

*Poem written by Tahli O., Gr. 4

IDEA FILE
a hopping bug
an octopus
sound waves
a bouncing ball
falling leaves
a secret
ocean waves
a pretzel
a juggler
a bothersome bee

angel wings
melting ice cream
music
a ski trail
a wild, winding river
swinging on a swing
a layered sandwich
footsteps
a pogo stick trail
a flock of birds

Use with page 89.

Name

WEATHERED WORDS

When Max goes out on an assignment to cover wild weather, his words become turbulent, too. They start taking the shape of lightning and tornadoes!

Choose one of the weather topics below and make a painted writing piece about it in the box. Make the shape of the writing match the topic.

FLASHING FINGERS OF JAGGED LIGHT CRACKLE THROUGH THE BLACKNESS AND SPLIT THE SKY.

rainstorm
blizzard
moving clouds
tornado
hurricane
tidal waves
mudslide
earthquake
soft snowflakes
wild wind
fat hailstones
avalanche

WITH THE ROAR OF A FREIGHT TRAIN, THE WHIRLING FUNNEL EATS AND CHURNS. EVERYTHING IN ITS PATH IS FRAGILE.

Use with page 88.

Name

Common Core Reinforcement Activities: 5th Grade Language

ASK ME ANYTHING!

If you want to find out something, you need to ask the right questions. Good reporters ask good questions. They plan their questions before they go investigating, so that they will know exactly what to ask.

Excuse me, sir. Do you speak English?

Nx. Vox ui Galactica?*

Think about the questions you would ask to find out interesting information about the people or events on pages 90 and 91. Get ready for some interviews by writing down the questions. Write clear, complete questions that ask exactly what you want to know! Write at least four good questions to ask each person or character.

1. a snake handler _____

2. a world record-holder _____

3. a peanut inspector _____

Use with page 91.

Name

No. Do you speak Galactica?

Get ready for some interviews by writing down the questions.
Write clear, complete questions that ask exactly what you want to know.

4. someone who's won an eating contest _____

EERP

_____

_____

_____

5. someone with a pet lion _____

_____

_____

_____

6. a cliff diver _____

_____

_____

_____

7. a rodeo clown _____

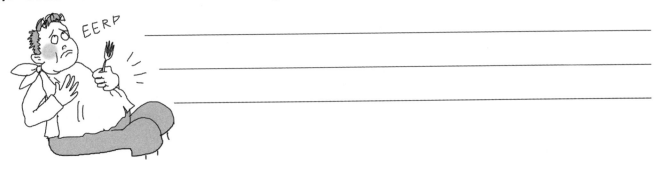

_____

_____

_____

Use with page 90.

Name _____

Common Core Reinforcement Activities: 5th Grade Language

WHAT CHARACTERS!

SPARK Magazine looked for contestants for a "Believe-It-or-Not!" contest. The magazine wanted to feature people who had done unusual or unbelievable things. The magazine placed an ad inviting people with special accomplishments to come in for an interview. To get ready to write articles, reporters began collecting interesting words that might help write about characters.

For each character on this page and page 93, write a list of words that could be used in a description. Use words from the lists on these two pages and try to add some words of your own.

peppy	rotund
suspicious	musical
athletic	insomniac
outrageous	fearless
adventurous	annoying
quirky	dependable
elderly	hilarious
eccentric	clever
limber	serious
offensive	stubborn
arrogant	mature
courageous	precocious
sleazy	massive
droopy	patient
cheerful	

1. owner of the world's smallest pony

2. person who's gone the longest time without sleep

3. holds the world paddleball-bounce record

4. the oldest skydiver in the country

Use with page 93.

Name

Create a name for each of the characters on pages 92 and 93.

comical	persistent
lazy	foolish
mean	rebellious
humble	reasonable
delightful	unreasonable
unpredictable	attractive
forgetful	joyous
wicked	sparkling
energetic	gloomy
miserable	mischievous
watchful	mysterious
talented	lonely
creative	reclusive
old-fashioned	jolly

1. _____
2. _____
3. _____
4. _____
5. _____
6. _____
7. _____
8. _____

Write a list of great words for describing each character. Then choose one of the eight characters and write a paragraph or two describing that character. You can pretend that you have interviewed the character. Do your writing on a separate piece of paper.

5. *grew a potato that looks like Abraham Lincoln*

_____
_____
_____
_____
_____
_____

6. *inventor of a machine that translates animal language*

_____
_____
_____
_____
_____
_____

7. *claims to be Elvis Presley*

_____
_____
_____
_____
_____
_____

8. *person who walks only on his hands*

_____
_____
_____
_____
_____
_____

Use with page 92.

Name _____

Common Core Reinforcement Activities: 5th Grade Language

PICTURE THIS

Keanu is a news photographer. He follows reporters around and gets the pictures to back up the stories. At the end of the day yesterday, some of his photos were lost. Interestingly, the reporter also lost one of her written pieces!

Where the photo is missing, read the article and re-create the picture. Where the writing is missing, write an article, poem, essay, story, or opinion to match the ideas shown in the picture.

Leonardo de Chimpa

1.

Again, a tightrope walker attempts to cross the Grand Canyon. Tomasina M. Balance took her first steps at noon on Thursday in what was the first attempt to cross the canyon this year. She balanced for forty-five minutes with a few breath-holding wobbles. Watching crowds took a deep breath of relief when she successfully completed the 5,000-foot walk. This feat came just months after she crossed over Niagara Falls where foggy air and flying birds challenged her every step.

2.

_____

_____

_____

_____

_____

_____

_____

_____

_____

_____

Name

STRAIGHT FROM THE PAGES

Stories are full of enticing characters, fascinating settings, surprising events, and great drama. Find a story (a short story, novel, or play) and see how the author presents these details! If you need help finding a story, ask your teacher, librarian, parent, or an adult.

Select a story. Choose a character, a setting, or an event from the story. Write a description that gives a clear picture of that character, setting, or event. Use details from the story.

Title of story _____

Name of character, setting, or event _____

Description

_____

_____

_____

_____

_____

_____

_____

_____

_____

_____

_____

_____

_____

_____

_____

Name _____

EVIDENCE, PLEASE!

Information is everywhere you look! Books, magazines, DVD's, the Internet, newspapers, apps on all kinds of devices—all are places you can go to learn just about anything! Take a close-up look at a presentation of information.

Select a sample of informational text. Choose a main point the author makes. Find evidence or reasons that the author uses to support the point. Describe the evidence in a paragraph.

Title and source of text_____

A main point is_____

_____

Evidence

_____

_____

_____

_____

_____

_____

_____

_____

_____

_____

_____

Evidence

_____

_____

_____

_____

_____

_____

_____

_____

_____

_____

_____

How to Feed an Alligator

THE BERMUDA TRIANGLE
FACT OR FICTION?

Black Holes—
What Are They?

Name

LANGUAGE

Grade 5

MAROONED AND TERRORIZED AND . . .

Alex is in trouble! He is marooned and terrorized and threatened and exhausted. To write about his situation, you will certainly need some conjunctions! *Conjunctions* connect words or groups of words. Some are single words. Some are two or three words. *Correlative conjunctions* link words or phrases of the same type.

Circle a conjunction in each sentence. Be ready to tell what words or phrases it connects.

1. Lorenzo's ship went down because it struck a reef.

2. Luckily, he had inflated the lifeboat before the ship sank.

3. He swam miles even though he was exhausted.

4. Lorenzo is in big trouble unless someone rescues him.

I'm sunburned and marooned on a deserted island surrounded by sharks and pirates and there's a storm coming!

Circle a pair of conjunctions in each sentence. Be ready to tell what words or phrases they connect.

5. Not only is Lorenzo tired, but also he is injured and hungry.

6. Neither the storm nor the shark scares him.

7. The shark is not as fierce as it looks.

8. He wonders whether the pirates will bother him or leave him alone.

Name

98

BON VOYAGE!

Bon Voyage! is what people say to someone leaving on a trip—especially a trip on the sea. It means *Good trip on the water.* The group of words "on the water" is a prepositional phrase that tells where the trip will be. The word *on* is the preposition. *Water* is the object of the preposition.

Look for prepositional phrases. Underline each one you find. Be ready to tell what purpose the prepositional phrase serves in the sentence. Circle the preposition and draw an arrow from it to the object of that preposition.

1. Sasha has already gone exploring below the deck.

2. She chose to have an adventure instead of dinner.

3. She found a secret passageway below Deck Four.

4. "That girl has gone off without my permission!" said Mom.

Fill in the blanks to finish the prepositional phrases. You may need to write a preposition or an object.

5. Sasha is snooping _____ the lifeboats.

6. Oh, no! She's climbed _____ some _____ !

7. Now, she is tiptoeing _____ the captain's wheel.

8. Sasha, you'll be in trouble because of your _____ !

Name _____

Common Core Reinforcement Activities: 5th Grade Language

YIKES!

Alex runs from a huge wave! Wow!
Is he surprised, excited, or terrified?
Some words are just right for close calls
or emergencies or exciting situations.
These are called *interjections*!

**Circle the interjection in each sentence.
(There may be more than one.) Be ready
to tell what purpose those words serve
in the sentence.**

1. Stop! You're headed for a cliff!

2. Oh! No! There's trouble ahead.

3. Good luck! You'll need it with
   all those sharks out there.

4. That was very close. Whew!

5. "Shh!" A crab is creeping up
   on Alex.

6. Is Alex in for a shock?
   Absolutely!

Write an interjection in each blank.

7. _____! I barely escaped
   that barracuda!

8. I am so glad you did. _____!

9. _____! That crab
   has caught my toe.

10. Here's how I feel about that
    slippery squid: _____!

11. Will you come to the beach
    again, Alex? _____!

Name _____

AFTER DARK

There's nothing quite like the beach at night! It's such fun to hang out and jump into a whole lot of activities different from daytime on the beach. Tonight looks like a perfect evening.

Verbs written in one of the perfect tenses (past, present, or future) describe action that has already happened or has begun to be finished in the future. They use *has, have,* or *had*.

Look at the verbs. Decide if they are perfect tense. Write *yes* or *no*.

_____ 1. The Bradley kids have danced around the fire twice.

_____ 2. Zoie has roasted at least 12 marshmallows.

_____ 3. Lucas will eat far more than that.

_____ 4. The guys in the boat will have caught 40 fish.

Write three short sentences about something from the picture. Use a past perfect, present perfect, or future perfect verb in each one.

5. _____

_____

6. _____

_____

7. _____

_____

Name _____

Common Core Reinforcement Activities: 5th Grade Language

WHAT'S HAPPENING?

The word *fudge* may have been taken from Captain Fudge, a seaman with a reputation for not telling the truth. In the past, he *fudged* on the truth. This means he did not tell the whole story!

Verbs such as *fudge* or *fudged* tell about when something happened. Verbs can also give you an idea of the order in which things happened or the condition of something.

Read Captain Fudge's "truths." Circle the verbs in the sentences on the left below. Then write a verb from one of those sentences to match each description on the right.

1. I caught a whale with my bare hands.

2. The sea is coming to me as I call it.

3. I was eating a sea monster. I will soon find another.

4. My chocolates will keep filling the ocean.

5. I have been harnessing the wind all day.

6. I am wrestling a shark at this moment.

7. The sea devoured my shack and got a stomach ache.

8. I shall never tell a lie.

Write a verb that tells something that

_____ a. started happening earlier and is still happening

_____ b. is happening right now

_____ c. is happening right now

_____ d. happened in the past

_____ e. happened in the past

_____ f. happened in the past

_____ g. happened in the past

_____ h. will happen in the future

_____ i. is happening now and will continue

_____ j. happened second

Name _____

A SHIFTING STORY

A few minutes ago, the octopus had the upper "hand" in this incident. Now the squid has the upper "tentacle" and the octopus is all tangled! The story shifts minute by minute! The verbs shift, too—depending on the story.

Most of the time, it is important to keep the same verb tense within a sentence or a paragraph. This is called keeping verb tenses *parallel*.
Do this unless there is a good reason to change (or shift) tenses.

Look at each of these sentences. Decide if the verb tenses are correct. If they are not, explain the problem and tell what to do to make verb tenses parallel.

Tangled up again !

1. Avoid that squid and you should swim away.

   Explain: _____

   _____

   Fix:_____

   _____

2. By the time I can get there to help you, it is too late.

   Explain: _____

   _____

   Fix:_____

   _____

3. I won't be swimming here any more, and you are not either.

   Explain: _____

   Fix:_____

4. Can that squid outswim you, or wasn't he that fast?

   Explain: _____

   Fix:_____

5. I see a black streak in the water. Was that hiding another squid?

   Explain: _____

   Fix:_____

Name _____

WATCH OUT, CRAB!

Sam was in for a shock when he sat down too close to a crab's home. "Take that, Sam!" was the crab's response.

In the sentence above, someone was talking to (addressing) Sam. The comma was used to set that address off from the rest of the sentence. Explore and explain the use of commas in more examples below.

Explain why each comma was used in the sentence.

1. No, the crab was not happy.

   _____

   _____

2. It's true, isn't it, that Sam was not happy either?

   _____

   _____

3. Until this incident, Sam liked crabs.

   _____

   _____

4. Where will you sit next time, Sam?

   _____

   _____

5. At the end of the day, Sam had a sunburn, a headache, and a sore toe.

   _____

   _____

   _____

   _____

Insert commas where they are needed.

6. Normally the crabs on this beach are smaller.

7. Down by the water's edge crabs chase each other.

8. After sunset we dig in the sand for crabs.

9. Lexie Jamal and Todd found the most crabs.

10. Hey why is it that crabs pinch people?

11. Abby do you know the answer?

12. Hobbling around the beach with a crab on his toe Alex looked quite silly.

Name _____

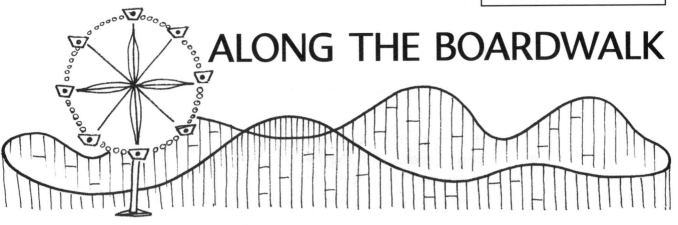

ALONG THE BOARDWALK

Walk along the boardwalk and enjoy all the sights and sounds.
Try out the great rides, delicious foods, and fun attractions.

**Read the sentences about some boardwalk attractions. Look for
commas. Are they used correctly? Are commas used every place
they should be? Write *yes* or *no*. If a comma is missing—insert it.
If it is in the wrong place—move it or cross it out.**

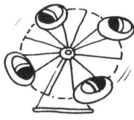

_____ 1. Don't forget to eat some pizza, ride the
roller coaster, and try some cotton candy.

_____ 2. Ordinarily, my first stop is the Arcade.

_____ 3. Then I ride *The Twister The Corkscrew*
and *The Screamin' Demon*.

_____ 4. Jonas what is the Fun House, really like?

_____ 5. Hey let's head for the flying airplanes next!

_____ 6. On the other side of the racetrack
you'll find the basketball toss.

_____ 7. Was that you hollering from the Ferris wheel,
Keesha?

_____ 8. It would be great to stop for a hot dog wouldn't it?

_____ 9. Yes I'd love a hot dog, or two.

_____ 10. Let's come back tomorrow, shall we?

Name _____

Common Core Reinforcement Activities: 5th Grade Language

BEACH READING

Gloria always takes some good reading material to the beach. Listen to what she has to say about her favorite things to read on the beach.

**Pay attention to the titles in the speech balloons.
Show that you know something about punctuating titles!
To each of the titles she mentions, add correct punctuation—
quotation marks or underlining (which is a substitute for italics).**

1.
The best beach book of all is Rap Singer Meets Sea Urchin.

2.
My favorite poem is Ode to the Seashore.

3.
I've just read the play The Lady and the Octopus.

4.
Deep Sea Mystery is the next book on my list.

5.
I need to finish my article, How to Act Like a Star.

6.
I've got a starring role in the movie Girl with the Golden Surfboard.

7.
Do you know the song, I'm Just a Hoarse Little Seahorse?

8.
My next singing album will be Underwater Melodies.

9.
Have you discovered the magazine, Secrets of the Starfish?

10.
Let's finish this article: How to be Glamorous Under Water.

Name _____

MISFITS IN THE SAND

Some words in the sand castles are spelled wrong.

Examine each castle carefully and cross out any misspelled words. Write the words correctly on the castles.

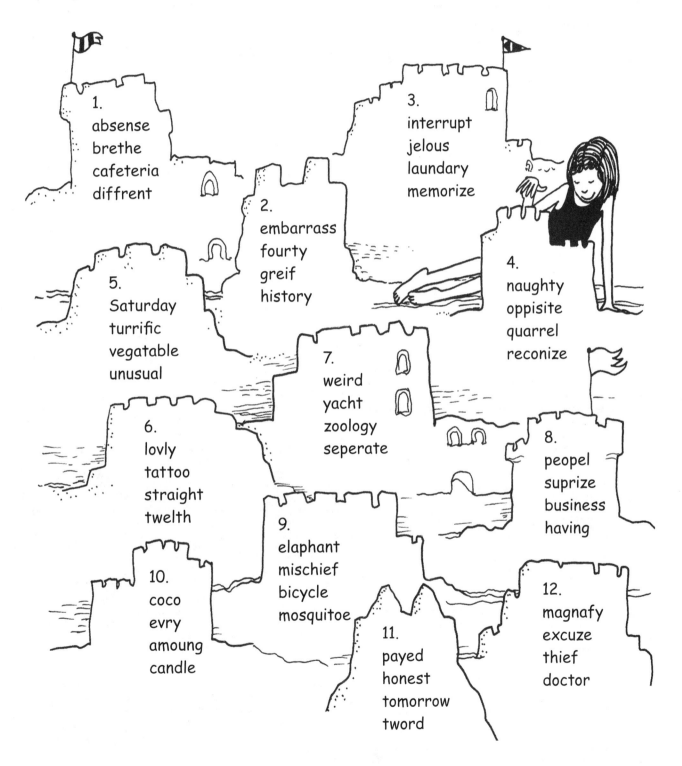

1.
absense
brethe
cafeteria
diffrent

2.
embarrass
fourty
greif
history

3.
interrupt
jelous
laundary
memorize

4.
naughty
oppisite
quarrel
reconize

5.
Saturday
turrific
vegatable
unusual

6.
lovly
tattoo
straight
twelth

7.
weird
yacht
zoology
seperate

8.
peopel
suprize
business
having

9.
elaphant
mischief
bicycle
mosquitoe

10.
coco
evry
amoung
candle

11.
payed
honest
tomorrow
tword

12.
magnafy
excuze
thief
doctor

Name _____

Common Core Reinforcement Activities: 5th Grade Language

TROUBLE IN THE SURF

Demi is staying on top of the waves quite well. It's a good thing, because there is trouble in those waves! The words have been tossed around and misspelled.

Write the correct spelling for each misspelled word in the surf.

1. acheve

2. niether

3. bisckit

4. occassionally

5. lisence

6. restarant

7. libary

8. performence

9. doller

10. lazer

11. chocalate

12. tougue

13. exercize

14. journy

15. pajammas

1. _____

2. _____

3. _____

4. _____

5. _____

6. _____

7. _____

8. _____

9. _____

10. _____

11. _____

12. _____

13. _____

14. _____

15. _____

Name _____

BEACH-BLANKET ERRORS

As George and Georgie rest in the sun, they think calm, restful thoughts.
It's too bad about the spelling errors!

**Each thought has at least one error. Cross out misspelled words
on the blankets and write them correctly in the spaces
below the blankets.**

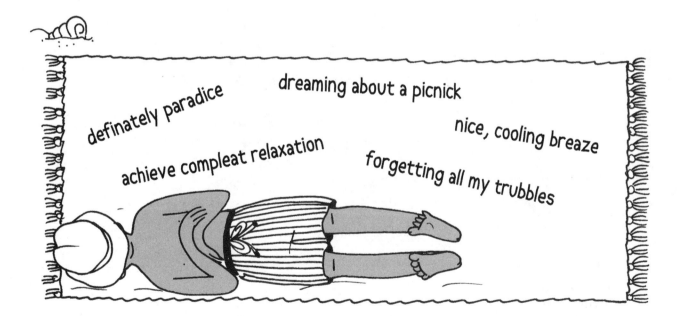

good excusse for a nap

lovly location

had enuf sunshine

never useing sunscreen

crab bitting my forth toe

definately paradice

dreaming about a picnick

nice, cooling breaze

achieve compleat relaxation

forgetting all my trubbles

Name

Common Core Reinforcement Activities: 5th Grade Language

SWIMMERS' LINE-UP

Seven eager swimmers wait to ride *The Twister*.

This sentence is one way to describe the scene below. But the sentence could be expanded or rearranged to change the style or meaning. Here are some examples:

- With great anticipation, eager swimmers line up for a chance to ride a heart-stopping roller coaster.
- Which of the seven swimmers is most eager to ride *The Twister*?
- Seven swimmers are out of the water. Now they'll ride the *Twister*.

Follow directions to adapt the sentences. Combine them, expand them, or rearrange them.

1. Expand this sentence to tell how the person feels about the experience she is about to have.
   ### Grandma has ridden roller coasters all her life.

   _____

   _____

2. Combine these sentences to make a more interesting sentence.
   ### Jojo can't wear his snorkel on the ride. Darian can't take his surfboard.

   _____

   _____

3. Rearrange this sentence to change the meaning.
   ### While waiting in line, a shark caught the swimmers' attention.

   _____

   _____

4. Rearrange this sentence to change the style of the writing.
   ### The wind picked up; the surf crept up on the people waiting in line.

   _____

   _____

Name _____

SHOP TALK

One customer at the swim shop says,

> "I'll try on
> a blue girl's swimsuit
> in size eight."

Another customer says,

> "I'll try on
> a girl's blue swimsuit
> in size eight."

Notice the difference between the meanings of the two statements! Then listen in on more customer comments and questions. Pay attention to the style and meaning of each one.

Follow directions to adapt the sentences. Combine them, expand them, or rearrange them.

1. Expand this sentence to make a more interesting sentence.
   "How does a person get into a wet suit, anyway?"

   _____

   _____

2. Rearrange this sentence to show that the sunscreen has the spray top.
   "Did you sell the last bottle of sunscreen
   to that customer with the spray top?"

   _____

   _____

3. Expand this sentence to show more clarity about what the customer wants.
   "I'm looking for some snorkeling gear that is a good price."

   _____

   _____

4. Rearrange or expand this sentence to change the style of the writing.
   "I sat in that raft and now it has a hole."

   _____

   _____

Name _____

Common Core Reinforcement Activities: 5th Grade Language

BEACH CONVERSATIONS

How interesting it is to eavesdrop on conversations at the beach today! Some of the language used is informal—just what you might expect to hear at the beach. But some of it is formal, and you might be surprised to hear it here.

Circle *formal* or *informal* for each bit of conversation. If you choose *formal*, rewrite (or say) the statement as it might be in more informal English. If you choose *informal*, rewrite (or say) the statement in formal English. Use a separate piece of paper.

1. Holy cow! Did ya get a look at that shark?   formal   informal

2. I would be so honored to participate in your class.   formal   informal

3. Hiya. How's it goin'?   formal   informal

4. Could you please pass me that bottle
   if it is not too much trouble?   formal   informal

5. You want me to do what??? No way!   formal   informal

6. It is so pleasant to make your
   acquaintance. I shall look forward
   to contacting you frequently in the future.   formal   informal

7. I'm sorry to inform you, sir, that at this very
   moment your umbrella is being snatched
   away by a menacing wave.   formal   informal

8. May I interest you in a chilled
   beverage at this time?   formal   informal

9. So, where do you live?   formal   informal

10. Stop it! You're a pest!   formal   informal

Name

HOT BEACH, COOL DRINKS

Ahhhhhh! A cool drink on a hot day! What happens when the sweaty sunbather gets a swallow of a cool, icy drink? The sentence will tell you!

**Guess what each bold word means from the way
it is used in the sentence. Write your guess on the line.
Then look up the word in the dictionary, and write
the actual meaning.**

1. A cool drink of lemonade **revived** the spirits of the sunbather.

   Guess: _____ Definition: _____

2. After the storm, the ocean was **turbid**—filled with dirt and mud.

   Guess: _____ Definition: _____

3. The weather report called for **variable** winds, so we weren't sure what to expect.

   Guess: _____ Definition: _____

4. The waves were so **hazardous** that the fishing boat had to return to the pier.

   Guess: _____ Definition: _____

5. It's easier to take a picture of a **stationary** boat than a moving one.

   Guess: _____ Definition: _____

6. Alisha was **morose** for weeks because the cast on her leg kept her from swimming.

   Guess: _____ Definition: _____

7. Jack has a **volatile** temper today. You don't know if he will be calm or furious.

   Guess: _____ Definition: _____

8. It was an **incredible** feat of strength for Grandma to wrestle the shark!

   Guess: _____ Definition: _____

9. Sandy's **uncouth** remarks offended everyone and got her in trouble with the lifeguard.

   Guess: _____ Definition: _____

10. The crab was so **minuscule** that Kate needed a magnifying glass to identify it.

    Guess: _____ Definition: _____

Name _____

Common Core Reinforcement Activities: 5th Grade Language

SUNKEN TREASURE

A treasure chest has been sitting on the bottom of the ocean for years. How did it get there? These words sank along with the treasure, but some words are missing from the tale!

Notice the bold words or phrases. Decide the meaning of each one by looking at how it is used in the sentence. Then choose a word from the chest or ocean bottom that fits the meaning. Write that word near the bold word in the sentence.

How Did the Treasure Get Here?

1. A crafty pirate pushed it overboard from his ship and **plotted** to get it later.

2. It was **propelled** onto an island by a **monumental** tidal wave.

3. Someone found it in a pirate's cave and threw it off a high **embankment** into the ocean.

4. The chest was picked up by a **cyclone** and dropped into the ocean.

5. It fell overboard when a ship was **flung** around in a wild **upheaval**.

6. Two divers **hauled** the chest off a beach at midnight and **stashed** it here.

7. It slid into the **briny deep** during a terrible **Earth tremor**.

8. A whale's tail **violently dislodged** it from the deck of a pirate **vessel**.

9. A pirate ship **splattered** against the rocks and **foundered** in a hurricane.

10. No one really knows how the chest got here. It is a huge **enigma**.

ocean washed storm earthquake hid

cliff shook bridge mystery crashed huge

tornado violent dragged sank ship tossed

intended

Name _____

HOW MANY WHALES?

Only four of the twenty whales are jumping today. Is this the *majority* of whales or the *minority*? There are many words that get confused with others because they have similar sounds, looks, spellings, or meanings.

**Each example below has a pair of words
that are often confused with each other.
Circle the correct word to answer each sentence.**

1. Four of the twenty whales are jumping today.
    Is this the **majority** or the **minority**?

2. Natalie's doctor told her that she has strep throat.
    Is this a **diagnosis** or a **prognosis**?

3. We'll cook our clam chowder over low heat for a long time.
    Will we let the soup **simmer** or **boil**?

4. Those flowers by the pier only last for one year, then they need to be replanted.
    Are they **annuals** or **perennials**?

5. Hannah won free surfing lessons for perfect attendance at school this year.
    Were the awards given by the **principle** or the **principal**?

6. Barb's mom just finished writing a children's story about manatees.
    Will she get a **copyright** or a **patent** for her book?

7. Three friends found a redwood tree. They measured it by reaching their arms around the trunk and holding each other's hands.
    Did they measure the **circumference** or the **diameter**?

8. A widespread storm with high winds brought huge waves crashing against the island.
    Was this a **tornado** or a **hurricane**?

9. I found some sea glass that light could pass through, but I couldn't see through it.
    Was this glass **transparent** or **translucent**?

10. The sailor offered to take our whole group to the island for free. We said, "Yes!"
    Did we **except** or **accept** his offer?

Name

Common Core Reinforcement Activities: 5th Grade Language

A BIPED ON A UNICYCLE

This **biped** on a **unicycle** is showing off his **biceps**
to the camera on a **tripod**. Your knowledge
of root meanings and prefix meanings should
help you decide the meanings of the bold words.

**Identify the roots, prefixes, and suffixes
in the bold words in each box. Use your
knowledge of their meanings to help you
decide what the words mean.
Then do the drawings!**

1. Draw an **octopus** riding a **tricycle**.	2. Draw some **binoculars** inside a **pentagon**.	3. Draw a **decapod** crawling on a **hexagon**.
4. Draw a **semicircle** inside a **quadrilateral**.	5. Draw a **hexapod** sleeping in a **heptagon**.	6. Draw a **triangle** inside a **nonagon**.

Name

116

SHARK ALERT

There are more than 400 different kinds of sharks! How many of them have you met?

Find out a fact about two of them. Choose a suffix from the rocks to make a word that matches each meaning. Write the boxed letters in order on the answer lines to discover the names of these two sharks.

This spotted shark can grow to be 6 feet long!

1. full of treachery [ ] _ _ _ _ _ _ _

2. someone who dives _ [ ] _ _ _

3. relating to magic _ _ [ ] _ _ _ _

4. to make deep _ _ _ [ ] _

5. to make afraid _ [ ] _ _ _ _ _ _

Answer: a _ _ _ _ _ _ shark

This shark lives along the shores of warm oceans near the mouths of rivers. Some even live in fresh water.

6. toward the sky _ _ _ [ ] _ _ _

7. full of hunger [ ] _ _ _ _ _ _

8. pertaining to the ocean _ _ [ ] _ _ _

9. able to break _ _ _ _ _ [ ] _

10. state of being sharp _ _ _ _ [ ] _ _

Answer: a _ _ _ _ _ shark

ward (toward)

ic (pertaining to)

ness (state of being)

en (to make)   *ous* (full of)   *able* (able to be)

er (one who)   *ry* (full of)   *al* (relating to)

Name _____

Common Core Reinforcement Activities: 5th Grade Language

COULD YOU? WOULD YOU? SHOULD YOU?

Could you float on a *catamaran*? Would you swim in a *maelstrom*? Should you dive into a *maw*? You can't answer these questions unless you know what the words mean!

Use a dictionary to find the meanings of the words in bold. Then write your answer to each question. Be ready to explain your answers!

1. Could you float on a **catamaran**? _____

2. Would you swim in a **maelstrom**? _____

3. Should you dive into a **maw**? _____

4. Could you catch a fish in a **coupe**? _____

5. Would you see a **manatee** at a **matinee**? _____

6. Should you bargain with a **barracuda**? _____

7. Could you sniff an **aroma** on the beach? _____

8. Would you give a **marimba** to a **mollusk**? _____

9. Should you **prevaricate** to the lifeguard? _____

10. Could you take a rest in a **bungalow**? _____

11. Would you be **cordial** to a **carnivore**? _____

12. Should you float into a **treacherous** current? _____

13. Could you float on a **foible**? _____

14. Would you enjoy listening to a **monotonous** song? _____

15. Should you **aggravate** an angry eel? _____

Name _____

WHAT WOULD YOU DO WITH IT?

Julianne has found an unusual use for a flounder! What would you do with a flounder?

Look at each of the words below. Circle the most reasonable thing to do with each of the items listed. You may need some help from your dictionary!

What would you do with a . . .

1. **flounder**?	use it as a bookmark	fry it for lunch	wear it on your head
2. **plankton**?	put it on a pizza	feed it to a fish	write a letter on it
3. **snorkel**?	live in it	take it swimming	fry it with bacon
4. **brooch**?	bury it	write to it	put it in a jewelry box
5. **scoundrel**?	tickle it	avoid it	water it
6. **grotto**?	explore it	color it red	make noise with it
7. **query**?	clean it with soap	plant it	find an answer to it
8. **rumba**?	mail it	dance it	dress it up
9. **soufflé**?	measure it	bake it	wear it to dinner
10. **trophy**?	show it off	melt it	sing to it
11. **banister**?	hold on to it	plant it	put frosting on it
12. **marimba**?	feed it	dance with it	make music on it
13. **foe**?	wrap it up	draw with it	make friends with it
14. **sophomore**?	send it to school	paint it	put it on a sandwich
15. **sieve**?	slice it	put it in the bank	pour water through it
16. **architect**?	boil it	hire it	put it in an envelope

Name

Common Core Reinforcement Activities: 5th Grade Language

HO HUM

Samantha's letter to her friend Bo is full of figurative language.

Circle all the examples of figurative language you can find in Samantha's letter. Look for metaphors, similes, idioms, and other "figures of speech." Be ready to identify what kind of figure of speech each example is. Be ready to explain and discuss the literal meaning of each example.

How many examples did you find?

_____

Dear Bo,

Ho, hum! What a dull, dull day! Here I sit in this new bathing suit that cost me an arm and a leg, with the sun beating on me, the waves pounding like drums, and the seagulls squawking as loud as a rock band. I love the beach—just like my dad. I'm a chip off the old block! The water and sky are as pretty as a picture.

I do love the beach, but nothing is happening! Yes, the crabs are racing around faster than greased lightning, but there's no real action! My day is as dry as dust and as dull as a doorknob.

If only something outrageous would happen, this could turn out to be a red-letter day. I wish a giant waterspout would go bananas across the ocean. Or I wish a lifeguard would blow her top and go off her rocker right in front of everyone. Or wouldn't it take the cake if a dreadful sea monster appeared in the water, breaking up ships like toothpicks? Just think of how people would go running down the beach, scared stiff and screaming bloody murder! And wouldn't it be the last straw if all this happened and I missed it because I was sleeping?

Well, some say, "Out of sight, out of mind," but I say that absence makes the heart grow fonder. I miss you. I wish I could just snap my fingers and you'd be here, quick as a wink! Make no bones about it, today is a wipe-out! If only you were here, then this day would not be deader than a doornail!

Love,
Samantha

Name _____

HAPPY AS A CLAM

Are clams really happy? How do you know? What does it mean when someone is "happy as a clam" or "mad as a wet hen"? These are examples of figurative language. They have a meaning that is a little different from what the words actually say.

At the beach picnic, all these friends and family members are using figurative language. Write what each saying really means! Then, on a separate sheet of paper, draw what each saying would look like if the words meant what they actually said!

_____

_____

_____

_____

_____

_____

_____

_____

Name _____

GOOD TASTE IN FRIENDS

What does it mean to have "good taste in friends"? Does it have anything to do with eating your friends? No! It's just an example of figurative language. The meaning is different from what the words actually say.

At the beach picnic, all these friends and family members are using figurative language. Write what each saying really means!

_____

_____

_____

_____

_____

_____

_____

_____

Name

THE BEACH CONNECTION

What's the connection between all this stuff left lying around on the beach?
The connection is **synonyms**.

Draw a path to help the crab get through the maze and across the beach to meet his friend. The path can only touch items that contain pairs of synonyms. You might need some help from your dictionary!

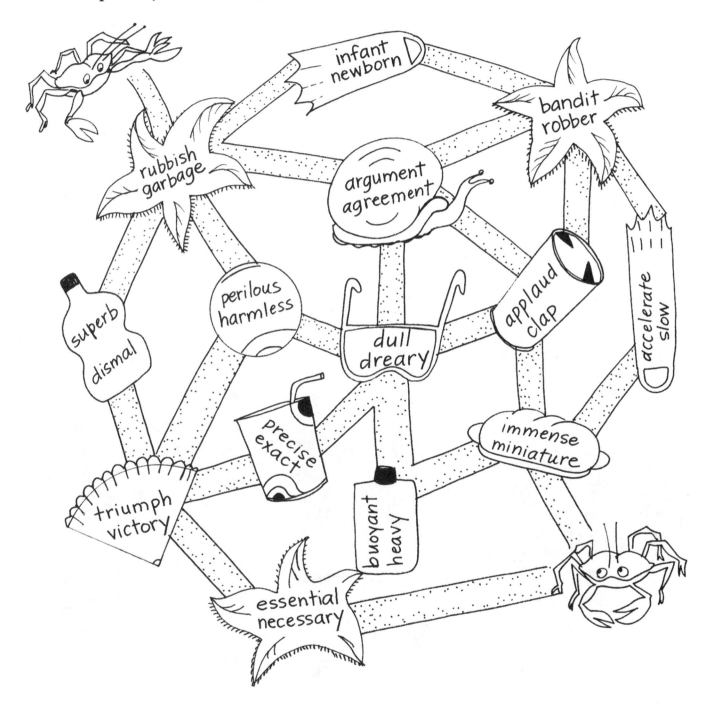

infant newborn

bandit robber

rubbish garbage

argument agreement

superb dismal

perilous harmless

dull dreary

applaud clap

accelerate slow

precise exact

immense miniature

triumph victory

buoyant heavy

essential necessary

DON'T OBEY THE SIGNS

Everything you can read on the beach below says the opposite of what it should!

Read each sign, label, and title. Look for one word that could be replaced with its opposite. Cross out that word and write its antonym to change the meaning of the message.

A WHALE OR A WAIL?

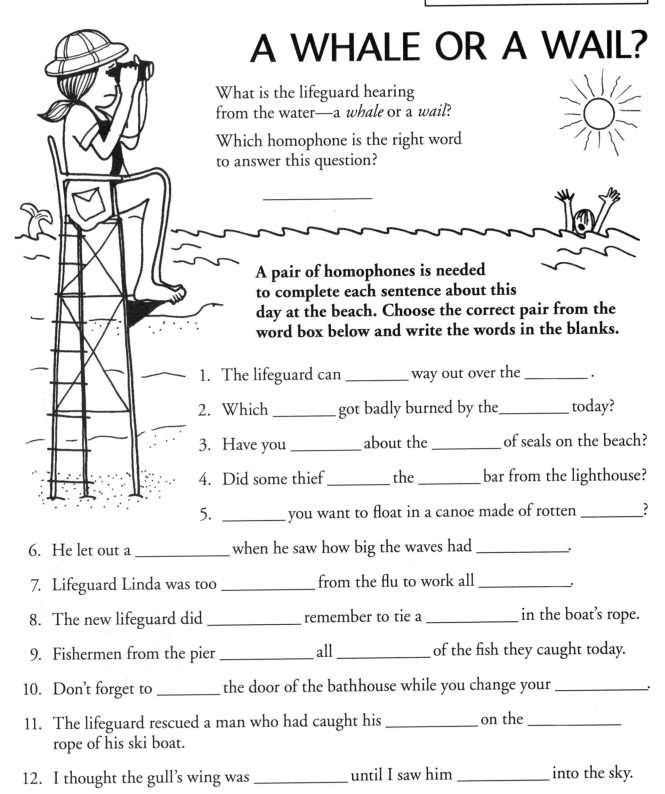

What is the lifeguard hearing from the water—a *whale* or a *wail*?

Which homophone is the right word to answer this question?

_____

A pair of homophones is needed to complete each sentence about this day at the beach. Choose the correct pair from the word box below and write the words in the blanks.

1. The lifeguard can _____ way out over the _____ .

2. Which _____ got badly burned by the_____ today?

3. Have you _____ about the _____ of seals on the beach?

4. Did some thief _____ the _____ bar from the lighthouse?

5. _____ you want to float in a canoe made of rotten _____?

6. He let out a _____ when he saw how big the waves had _____.

7. Lifeguard Linda was too _____ from the flu to work all _____.

8. The new lifeguard did _____ remember to tie a _____ in the boat's rope.

9. Fishermen from the pier _____ all _____ of the fish they caught today.

10. Don't forget to _____ the door of the bathhouse while you change your _____.

11. The lifeguard rescued a man who had caught his _____ on the _____ rope of his ski boat.

12. I thought the gull's wing was _____ until I saw him _____ into the sky.

see	sea	heard	herd	not	knot
groan	grown	steal	steel	ate	eight
son	sun	would	wood	close	clothes
sore	soar	weak	week	toe	tow

Name _____

Common Core Reinforcement Activities: 5th Grade Language

MAKING WAVES

It's a huge wave! The biggest waves
in the world are caused by earthquakes.
What is this kind of wave called?

**Find its name and the other answers
in the word bank to solve the puzzle.**

WORD BANK

fjord	weed
tsunami	sea
ichthyologist	mariner
habitat	archipelago
ecology	trough
grotto	abalone
flotsam	

DOWN

1. a shell lined with mother-of-pearl
2. the study of natural environments
3. natural setting where an animal lives
4. a cave
7. a tidal wave
8. a sailor
10. kelp is a kind of sea_____

ACROSS

5. the lowest point in a wave
6. a scientist who studies fish
9. floating wreckage
11. a group of islands
12. a long, narrow inlet of the sea between
tall, rocky cliffs
13. the ocean

Name

ASSESSMENT
AND
ANSWER KEYS

Language Arts & Literacy Assessment...**128**

    Part One: Reading.. 128

    Part Two: Writing... 133

    Part Three: Language A—Conventions 135

    Part Four: Language B—Vocabulary 137

Assessment Answer Key **139**

Activities Answer Key **140**

LANGUAGE ARTS & LITERACY ASSESSMENT

PART ONE: READING

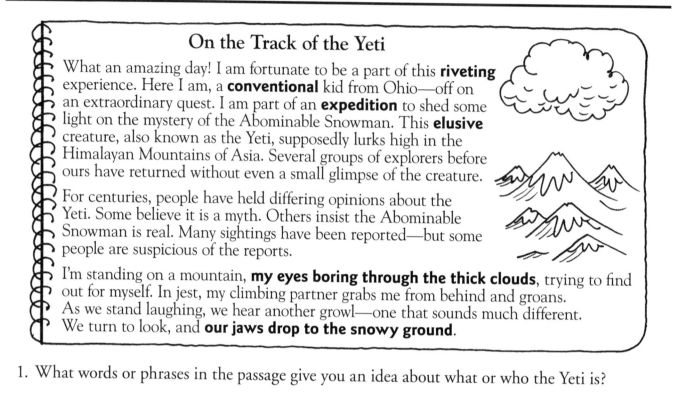

On the Track of the Yeti

What an amazing day! I am fortunate to be a part of this **riveting** experience. Here I am, a **conventional** kid from Ohio—off on an extraordinary quest. I am part of an **expedition** to shed some light on the mystery of the Abominable Snowman. This **elusive** creature, also known as the Yeti, supposedly lurks high in the Himalayan Mountains of Asia. Several groups of explorers before ours have returned without even a small glimpse of the creature.

For centuries, people have held differing opinions about the Yeti. Some believe it is a myth. Others insist the Abominable Snowman is real. Many sightings have been reported—but some people are suspicious of the reports.

I'm standing on a mountain, **my eyes boring through the thick clouds**, trying to find out for myself. In jest, my climbing partner grabs me from behind and groans. As we stand laughing, we hear another growl—one that sounds much different. We turn to look, and **our jaws drop to the snowy ground**.

1. What words or phrases in the passage give you an idea about what or who the Yeti is?

   _____

   _____

2. Describe the difference between the narrator's view of the Yeti and his climbing partner's view.

   _____

   _____

3. What is the theme of this passage? _____

Tell the meaning of each word or phrase as it is used in the passage.

4. riveting _____

   _____

5. conventional _____

   _____

6. quest _____

   _____

7. elusive _____

   _____

8. my eyes boring through the thick clouds_____

   _____

   _____

9. our jaws drop to the snowy ground _____

   _____

Name _____

128

Only the Night Knows

Hiding in the deep tree-cast shadows
Silent viewer watches dark figure
Watches as she creeps across the balcony,
Her tiptoe steps soft as air.
The dark asks for complete hush.
Any sound would be like crashing thunder splitting the night.
Smoothly she scales the edge
Ties her cherished bundle to snakelike rope
Lowers it to the ground with gentle care,
Then eases herself as cautiously and soundlessly
Over the balcony, down the slender rope after the bundle.
In a fragment of a moment, she ties the bundle around her waist
And evaporates into the dark tangled arms of the vines.
Eyes follow until the darkness swallows her,
Quiet watcher making no move.
Only the wide eyes of the night know her name or mission.

10. What is the theme of the passage?

_____

_____

_____

11. What is the meaning of *scales* in line 7?

_____

_____

_____

12. What is the meaning of *cherished* in line 8?

_____

_____

_____

13. Around which of these structures would
    you say the passage is formed?

   a. a problem and solution

   b. a comparison

   c. a sequential story

   d. a series of questions

   e. a reversed time sequence

   f. questions and answers

14. Identify two similes in the passage:

_____

_____

_____

_____

15. Identify one other metaphor in the passage:

_____

_____

_____

16. Write a brief summary of the poem.

_____

_____

_____

_____

_____

_____

_____

_____

_____

_____

Name

An extreme sport called *caving* is not for everyone. But some daring adventurers travel deep into the earth to explore **regions** that few people ever see.

Cavers take special equipment for their trips into deep caves. Each explorer needs three or more **reliable** sources of light, a helmet, good boots and gloves, and special clothing. On some trips, climbing equipment is needed. If cavers plan to explore underground rivers or pools, they may also carry scuba equipment or inflatable rafts and paddles.

uh oh

Inside the caves, explorers face many dangers. Some cavers get lost and are not able to find their way out. Others die from falls, drowning, **hypothermia**, or shortage of oxygen.

Why do cavers get involved in such a **precarious** sport? For many, it is challenging to **venture** into places that are hidden from most visitors. Others are hoping to find treasure. Still others appreciate the beauty of the caves. And some just enjoy the thrill of a dangerous adventure. Whatever the reasons, the sport is more than just an adventure. It is extremely risky business.

17. Write two key ideas from the text. For each, write two supporting details.

Idea: _____   Idea: _____

_____   _____

Detail:_____   Detail:_____

_____   _____

Detail:_____   Detail:_____

_____   _____

18. The author says that "the sport is more than just an adventure." Circle evidence the author gives to support that idea.

19. Choose two of the bolded words. Decide the meanings from their context.

_____

_____

_____

_____

_____

Name

Common Core Reinforcement Activities: 5th Grade Language

April 10

Dear Frankie,

I should have known that you would grow up to be a frogman! You always loved hearing Grandpa Swamp's stories about his escapades as a Navy Seal. But even so, I am disturbed by this news that you are preparing to work as a scuba diver. I cannot forget what happened to your grandfather.

Please, make sure your training is good. Follow all the rules. Take several classes. Most scuba injuries and deaths are caused by human mistakes.

There are so many dangers. Watch out for rocks and coral—which can impair your equipment and your body. Don't nose around barracudas or sharks. Always stay with your partner. Don't venture into underwater caves!

You could be carried away from the boat or your partner by strong currents. You could descend too fast and suffer brain damage. You could get hypothermia and lose your senses. Underwater pressure can cause dangerous drowsiness.

Maybe you could find some other, safer sport. Why don't you try soccer?

Love,
Your worried mom

The Possible Dangers of Scuba Diving
- pain and damage to inner ear from fast descent
- decompression sickness, possibly fatal
- impaired judgment from nitrogen absorption
- oxygen toxicity at deep levels
- bursting lungs from too rapid ascent
- dangers from sea animals, such as sting rays
- faulty or broken equipment

Dangers can be greatly reduced with
- good training
- reliable safety procedures
- good, safe equipment
- diving with others

21. What is the meaning of *escapades* in line 2?

_____

_____

_____

_____

_____

20. How are the two passages different in the way the ideas about scuba diving are presented?

22. How do the two writers differ in their viewpoint about scuba diving?

_____   _____

_____   _____

_____   _____

_____   _____

_____   _____

_____   _____

Name _____

Common Core Reinforcement Activities: 5th Grade Language

23. Circle any word with an ending that sounds like *eyes*.

energize	revise	emphasis
supervise	surprise	device
criticize	promise	surmise

24. Circle any word with an ending that sounds like *eight*.

educate	chocolate	estimate
favorite	celebrate	rotate
definite	illiterate	fortunate

25. Circle any words that have prefixes.

practical	preview	pressure
coauthor	difference	acrobat
actor	exhale	semicircle

26. Circle words that have suffixes.

virtual	fatal	nonsense
argument	mistake	deflate
apology	generous	perform

27. Which word in the detective's light is pronounced: **prees-ice**? _____

28. Which word in the detective's light is pronounced: **dye-uh-ree**? _____

29. Which word in the detective's light is pronounced: **pur-cent**? _____

30. Which word in the detective's light is pronounced: **dee-surt**? _____

deserve   distress   dairy
dude   precise
percent   precede   dewy
dreary   dessert
diary   present

Decide if each pair of words shares the same root. If so, write the meaning of the root. If not, write *no*.

31. expel   repellent   _____

32. citation   civilian   _____

33. motion   mortal   _____

34. sonar   supersonic   _____

35. dissect   section   _____

36. territory   terminate   _____

37. reform   formation   _____

38. lunar   luminous   _____

39. annual   anonymous   _____

40. autograph   hieroglyphics   _____

Name _____

PART TWO: WRITING

1. Choose one of the pictures below to inspire a tall tale. Write your tale. Include a good title, a catchy beginning that communicates the main idea of the piece, clear details to tell about the event, and a strong ending. Be sure to exaggerate!

_____

(title)

_____

_____

_____

_____

_____

_____

_____

_____

_____

_____

_____

_____

_____

Name _____

Common Core Reinforcement Activities: 5th Grade Language

2. Write a short opinion piece about something you feel should be changed. It could be something in your school, town, or neighborhood, or something about movies, books, pop culture, or the Internet. Make a clear point. Add a few details to show how passionate you feel about this.

_____

_____

_____

_____

_____

_____

_____

3. Read about alligator wrestling. Then write a list of steps you think someone should follow to wrestle an alligator.

Alligator wrestling began as a hunting expedition for Native Americans. Now it has become a sport for thrill seekers. There are places where you can pay $100 to try your hand at wrestling an alligator. Don't count on any insurance at these places!

Some alligator farms now host alligator wrestling competitions. Wrestlers spend 10 minutes in pool with an alligator and hope that the alligator is not the victor.

_____

_____

_____

_____

_____

_____

_____

_____

_____

Name

PART THREE: LANGUAGE A—Conventions

1. Circle the conjunctions. Underline any correlative conjunctions.
   a. Bud became a pirate even though his dad told him not to.
   b. He signed up on the Black Diamond before he was ten.
   c. His dad protested, but the pirate lure was too strong.
   d. Neither the wild seas nor the hard work worries him.

2. Circle the preposition. Draw a line to its object.
   a. He's already explored around the whole ship.
   b. Don't set sail without your pirate boots, Bud!
   c. "I've got everything except the hat," he says.
   d. "Aye, aye," he shouts into the wind.

3. Insert an interjection into each blank.
   a. _____! Is that really a pirate?
   b. Turn the ship around! _____!
   c. Are they gaining on us? _____!

Look for any verb shifts in these examples. Cross out and fix verbs.

4. Avoid pirate ships and you should sail away.

5. Did you leave your jewelry at home? I hope you think of that.

6. I'm not sure that pirate looks friendly. What did you think?

7. How fast is this ship? I hope it was faster than that black-flagged ship.

---

8. Circle the sentence with a verb that tells something that began in the past and is still happening.
   a. As of next week, she will have been in pirate training for three years.
   b. Yes, she was a superb student!
   c. The next step will be piloting a ship.
   d. What were those crossbones for?

9. Circle verbs in perfect tense.
   a. Pirates have sailed this sea for decades.
   b. Will we see pirates here in the future?
   c. Black Bart will go down in history.
   d. Has Captain Hook always had a hook?
   e. Captain Jack has always been my favorite.

Name _____

Common Core Reinforcement Activities: 5th Grade Language

10. The raft trip is a disaster. So are the spellings of some of the words. Write each misspelled word correctly.

_____

_____

_____

_____

_____

_____

_____

_____

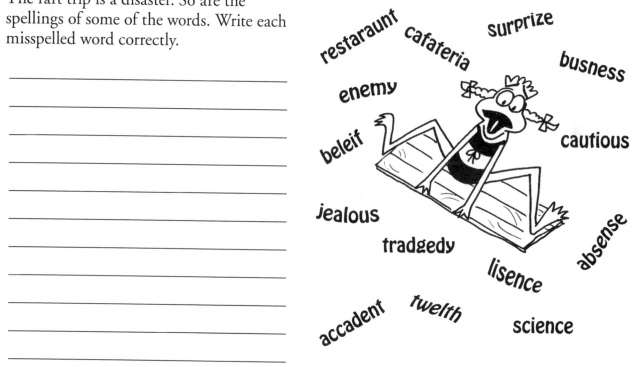

restaraunt   cafateria   surprize   busness   enemy   beleif   cautious   jealous   tradgedy   lisence   absense   accadent   twelth   science

11. Which titles are not punctuated correctly? Circle the letters. Tell how to correct them.

   a. movie   *The Last Barracuda*_____

   b. article   How to Live on Seaweed _____

   c. book   "Help! The Diary of a Castaway"_____

   d. magazine   <u>The Beach Lover's Travel Guide</u>_____

   e. ship   *Sea Fever*_____

Place commas correctly in these sentences from Fran's book.

12. Readers plan to visit these ten world wonders.

13. Ordinarily I recommend that you begin in Antarctica.

14. After you've seen the Taj Mahal ride a train across India.

15. You must see the Eiffel Tower my dear.

16. Oh yes that's the best travel advice I've had.

17. Stop in Anchorage Siberia Timbuktu and Khartoum.

18. After that take a sailboat to Madagascar.

19. Now that was a great introduction wasn't it?

Name

PART FOUR: LANGUAGE B—Vocabulary

loneliness hopeful

PIGLETS homeward terrify

friendless wooden actor

**Write a word from the bottle
with a suffix that means:**

1. one who _____

2. cause to be _____

3. without _____

4. small _____

5. made of _____

**Add a prefix to form a word
that fits the meaning shown.**

6. _____ operate (work together)

7. _____ approve (not approve)

8. _____ human (above human)

9. _____ hale (breathe out)

10. _____ freeze (against freezing)

**Circle the meaning of the bold word
in the sentence.**

11. Only a **robust** athlete would have the
endurance to ride that 50-foot wave.
   a. beginning
   b. strong
   c. tired
   d. experienced
   e. foolish
   f. Olympic

Answer *yes* or *no*.

_____ 12. Should you **prevaricate** about
whether or not you can swim?

_____ 13. Could you cook a **bungalow**?

_____ 14. Would you **aggravate** a grumpy
shark?

_____ 15. Should you put gravy
on a **sophomore**?

_____ 16. Could you wear a **manatee**?

**Circle the meaning of the bold word
in the sentence.**

17. After crashing beneath a wave, the surfer
lay **inert** on the beach for several minutes
before lifting her head off the sand.
   a. flat
   b. resting
   c. crooked
   d. motionless

**Find a word from the list
having a root to match
each meaning. Write
the letter.**

18. ____ earth

19. ____ high

20. ____ time

21. ____ water

22. ____ power

23. ____ break

24. ____ year

25. ____ move

26. ____ flee

A. aqueduct
B. fracture
C. arachnaphobia
D. fugitive
E. temporary
F. annual
G. flammable
H. descend
I. geology
J. lunar
K. solar
L. acrobat
M. dynamite
N. transfer
O. autograph

Name _____

Common Core Reinforcement Activities: 5th Grade Language

Describe the relationship between the two bold words in each sentence.

27. The crab looked **miniscule** next to the **immense** beached whale.

_____

28. A **mob** gathered to see the sight. "Where did this **horde** come from?" asked Lou.

_____

29. The crab **rode** on the whale as volunteers **rowed** the whale back out to sea.

_____

Circle the meaning of the bold word.

30. A young surfer survived so many horrible accidents that he began to believe he was **immortal**.

   a. honorable   c. very wise

   b. lucky   d. able to live forever

Circle the meaning of the bold word.

31. Everyone stared at Ev, who looked **conspicuous** wearing a parka while surfing.

   a. confused   c. standing out

   b. unnoticeable   d. fashionable

Each sign on the beach contains a figure of speech. On the line with the matching number, write the meaning of the statement on each sign.

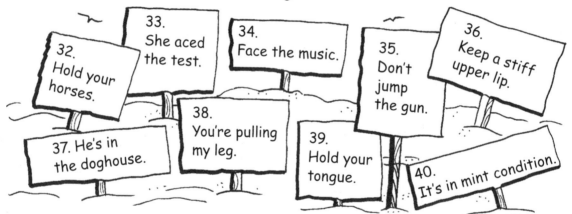

32. Hold your horses.
33. She aced the test.
34. Face the music.
35. Don't jump the gun.
36. Keep a stiff upper lip.
37. He's in the doghouse.
38. You're pulling my leg.
39. Hold your tongue.
40. It's in mint condition.

32. _____
33. _____
34. _____
35. _____
36. _____
37. _____
38. _____
39. _____
40. _____

Name

ASSESSMENT ANSWER KEY

Part One: Reading

Many answers will vary. Allow answers that adequately fulfill the instructions and can be justified by student if asked.

1. elusive creature, lurks high in the Himalayan Mountains, without even a small glimpse of the creature, some believe it is a myth, many sightings have been reported, growl
2. narrator is open to believing in the Yeti and wants to see one; partner is not a believer.
3. excitement about an adventure, anticipation, uncertainty
4. thrilling, fascinating
5. ordinary
6. search
7. hard to find or capture
8. I am looking hard through the clouds.
9. We are shocked.
10. mystery, secrecy, stealth
11. climbs
12. precious; valued
13. c
14. Answers will vary: steps soft as air; like crashing thunder splitting the night
15. Answers will vary: dark asks for complete hush; wide eyes of night know her name, darkness swallows her, tangled arms of the vines
16. Summaries will vary. An unknown person watches as a female figure quietly crosses a balcony, lowers a bundle and herself to the ground, and disappears into the vines. No one knows who she is or what she is doing.
17. Ideas identified and details will vary. Check to see that ideas identified are key, and

that details support them. (Ideas: Caving takes special equipment. Cavers face dangers. People choose caving for different reasons.)
18. Explorers face many dangers. Some cavers get lost. Others die.
19. regions—areas; reliable—trustworthy; hypothermia—dangerous condition where body temperature falls too low; precarious—dangerous; venture—trip or adventure or exploration
20. Answers will vary. One structure is a letter; the other is a poster or list-form. One presents building argument. One just gives information about dangers followed by ways to balance or avoid dangers.
21. adventures
22. The first writer is obviously worried and skeptical about the scuba diving. The second does not show any personal feelings—is more objective—stating dangers but giving a balanced view.
23. energize, revise, supervise, surprise, criticize, surmise
24. educate, estimate, celebrate, rotate
25. preview, coauthor, acrobat, exhale, semicircle
26. virtual, fatal, argument, apology, generous
27. precise
28. diary
29. percent
30. dessert
31. push (pel)
32. no
33. no
34. sound (son)
35. cut or divide (sect)

36. no
37. shape (form)
38. no
39. no
40. no

Part Two: Writing

1 through 3: Student writing will differ. Check all passages to see that they are clear and flow smoothly—and that they follow the directions adequately.

Part Three: Language A– Conventions

1. a. Circle: *even though*;
   b. Circle: *before*;
   c. Circle: *but*.
   d. Underline: *Neither . . . nor*
2. a. Circle: *around*—draw a line to ship;
   b. Circle: *without*—draw a line to boots;
   c. Circle: *except*—draw a line to hat;
   d. Circle: *into*—draw a line to wind.
3. Interjections will vary.
4. Cross out word *should*.
5. Change *think* to *thought*.
6. Change *did* to *do*.
7. no verb shifts
8. a
9. a. have sailed;
   d. Has...had;
   e. has...been
10. absence, cafeteria, restaurant, license, belief, surprise, twelfth, business, tragedy, accident
11. b—needs quotation marks; c—should be underlined or italicized
12. after *Readers*
13. after *Ordinarily*
14. after *Mahal*
15. after *Tower*
16. after *yes* (may also insert comma after *Oh*)

17. after *Anchorage, Siberia,* and *Timbuktu*
18. after *that*
19. after *introduction*

Part Four: Language B– Vocabulary

1. actor
2. terrify
3. friendless
4. piglets
5. wooden
6. cooperate
7. disapprove
8. superhuman
9. exhale
10. antifreeze
11. b
12. no
13. no
14. no
15. no
16. no
17. d
18. I
19. L
20. E
21. A
22. M
23. B
24. F
25. N
26. D
27. opposites (antonyms)
28. similar meanings (synonyms)
29. same sound but different meanings (homophones)
30. d
31. c
32. Wait! Be patient.
33. She scored well.
34. Take the consequences.
35. Don't start too soon.
36. Show courage.
37. He's in trouble.
38. You're teasing me.
39. Keep quiet.
40. It's in great condition.

ACTIVITIES ANSWER KEY

Note: There are many cases in which answers may vary. Accept an answer if student can give a reasonable justification or details to support it, or if you can see the sense in it.

Reading: Literature (pages 22–44)

pages 22–23

Answers may vary. Allow any reasonable meanings.

1. escapades
2. soar
3. antics
4. fraternize
5. scrutinize
6. endeavor
7. venture
8. probe, comb, snoop
9. fantasy, mythical
10. great, colossal, lavish
11. culinary
12. scale
13. treacherous
14. mythical, fantasy
15. ancient
16. foreboding
17. colossal
18. lavish
19. unfathomable
20. future
21. elusive
22. legendary
23. ruins
24. bargain
25. engage
26. gander
27. remote
28. fiercest

page 24

Answers may vary. Allow any reasonable meanings.

1. awful
2. excited, joyful
3. cave
4. reached
5. regret
6. soggy, damp
7. risky, dangerous
8. stay away from
9. interfere with, stop
10. complaining
11. evil, threatening, scary
12. worry, bother

page 25

Answers may vary. Allow any reasonable meanings.

1. prove, verify
2. make, allow; useless
3. give
4. use
5. eating
6. greasy
7. trash
8. forbidden
9. pay attention to; spread widely
10. not allowed
11. mess with
12. too much; scolded, punished
13. tickets
14. right away; end

page 26

Check for accurate supporting references to text circled in color.

1. RED: Giorgio's
2. BLUE: drawings for airplane, helicopter, human anatomy; Leonardo was a scientist, sculptor, architect, mathematician, military advisor, engineer.
3. GREEN: Drawings and notes
4. BLACK: drawing, sculpting
5. YELLOW: *The Last Supper*
6. ORANGE: Georgio's

page 27

1. 3, 1, 6, 5, 2, 4
2. 2, 5, 4, 3, 8, 1, 7, 6
3. 2, 4, 7, 1, 3, 5, 6

page 28

1. The Paleo-lyths
2. You're As Cuddly As a Woolly Mammoth
3. I Dino If I Love You Anymore
4. Be a Little Boulder, Honey
5. The Cave Dudes
6. I've Cried Pebbles over You
7. Terri Dactyl
8. The Cro-Magnon Crooners
9. The Petro Cliff Trio
10. The Hard Rock Arena
11. Dancin' at the Quarry
12. after dark
13. The Standing Stones

page 29

Answers will vary.

1. YELLOW: slipped another cut into the dancing air; lightning sharp knife; stabbed the sea
2. BLUE: roaring; moaning
3. RED: slipped; stabbed
4. ORANGE: angry; dancing; wailed; wind's feet; could not say another word
5. GREEN: feet could not take another step; tired as it was; could not say another word
6. PURPLE: could no longer hold the towering mountains on its back

page 30

Answers will vary. Theme may be something such as: being careful and working hard but taking risks. Check summaries to see that the main ideas are captured succinctly and clearly.

page 31

Answers will vary. Theme may be: mystery, watchfulness, or unsolved mystery. Check summaries to see that the main ideas are captured succinctly and clearly.

page 32

Answers will vary. Check summaries to see that the information gathered is presented succinctly.

1. Jewels are stolen, and there are at least two possible suspects.
2. Raw meat was stolen and most evidence points to the dog.
3. Sherlock has collected evidence, but no suspects stand out yet.

page 33

Answers will vary. Theme may be something like: A kayaker is in competition with the water and rocks, which want to get the better of him or her. Check summaries to see that the main ideas are captured succinctly and clearly.

pages 34–35

Answers will vary. Check to see that appropriate supporting evidence from the text is circled.

1. Count struts; Countess floats. Count is conceited; Countess is soft and sincere.
2. Both seem to be having fun.
3. This can vary. She might be like most like Count Pompous, because both are self-centered.
4. Prince Mischief and the dowager are opposites. He's all fun; she's all seriousness and propriety.
5. He might suggest that she relax and eat and be more agreeable.

page 36

Answers will vary. Judgments should be supported by good reasoning and evidence from the text.

page 37

Answers will vary.

1. Lines have a consistency and repetition, telling things that you can do with magic. Most start with a verb and active phrase.
2. Students may point out that the repetition emphasizes and builds message of the many things you can do with magic.

pages 38–39

Author purpose may vary. Check to see that answers are supported by evidence from the text.

1. c; *Purpose:* to give some history about Talula's singing career and background about her.
2. a; *Purpose:* to tell how hard it is to get to be a country music star.
3. b; *Purpose:* to advertise or inform of a new hit song.
4. b; *Purpose:* to explain how neon lights work.

page 40

Answers will vary. Look for evidence from the text to support answers to #1.

page 41

Answers will vary. Look for evidence from the text to support answers to #1.

pages 42–43

Answers will vary.

1. It is written in prose; the second passage is poetry.
2. "Thirteen Thrills" explains the science of a roller coaster ride. "Only for the Brave" tells how scary the roller coaster ride is and gives warnings.
3. Both have the same topic. Both show some awe of the roller coaster.
4. One is instructive, the other is cautionary.
5. Paragraphs add seriousness to the informational text of the first passage. The short lines and rhyme put the information

into a fun form that supports the warning tone and the message that your body is jerked around.

page 44

Comments will vary. As students discuss similarities and differences, look for reasoned evidence from text to support their ideas.

Reading: Informational Text (pages 46–68)

page 46

Answers may vary. Check to see that reasoning supports the answer and uses evidence from the text.

1. S. Snoop (greatest number of solved cases)
2. paranormal cases (lowest number total)
3. break-ins (greatest number total)
4. bank robberies (greatest number solved)
5. paranormal (solved more of these than anyone else or anything else)

page 47

Answers may vary. Check to see that reasoning supports the answer and uses evidence from the text.

1. No—surfer was caught, but arrest was not mentioned; no arrest was mentioned in the boa constrictor case.
2. Yes, Case 3 mentions clues; Cases 1, 2, and 4 infer clues
3. Pearls were missing (so the title of the case says) and, according to the illustration, were

found inside a piggy bank. It seems that a suspect, who had coins, may have been near the piggy bank to store the pearls there.

page 48

A. 40 days (step 4)
B. dries it out (step 4)
C. 20 or more (step 6)
D. organs (step 2)
E. brain (step 1)
F. putting it in 3 coffins (step 7)
G. Answers will vary. Check student explanation to see that it is substantiated by the text.

page 49

Check to see that circled text provides evidence for student answer choices.

1. Day 2 (possibly Day 3 also)
2. Day 1, Day 5
3. visibility, slippery track, feeling wet and cold, dealing with wind
4. Day 2, 3, 4
5. perhaps suspend the race

page 50

Ideas will vary. Check to see that the idea is central to the paragraph. Check circled details to see that they support the key idea the student identified.

1. The *Titanic* was the biggest and most luxurious ship ever built up to that time.
2. The ship struck an iceberg, and there were not enough lifeboats for all passengers.
3. The ship sank so fast and help did not come until the next day. Many passengers did not survive.

4. It is hoped that the exploration of the *Titanic* wreckage will help to solve some mysteries about why it sank.

page 51

Summaries will vary. Watch for accurate circling of key ideas and details in each paragraph.

1. Sammy and his Ma talk about sneaking a file to Louis in jail.
2. Maxie reveals that she doesn't have the "loot" that she is supposed to bring to the gang.
3. Harry makes arrangements for a secret delivery of a pizza.
4. Shorty tells a partner-in-crime not to rent a car for the getaway in a planned crime.

page 52

Key ideas, details, and summaries will vary. Check to see that details are from the text and that they support key ideas.

page 53

Answers and summaries will vary. Check to see that details are from the text and that they support key ideas.

page 54

1. waves
2. crest
3. trough
4. current
5. dissolved salts
6. tides
7. Earth, moon, sun
8. continental slope
9. benthos
10. plankton

page 55

Across
2. two
8. Constitution
9. laws

12. amend
13. senator
Down
1. Congress
3. Rhode Island
4. judicial
5. president
6. balances
7. population
10. three
11. veto

pages 56–57

Answers will vary.

1. They both give information about the International Space Station. They are both interesting—with things reader may not know.
2. One is an advertising brochure—very visual. It has short lines and phrases. The other is written in paragraph form.
3. The first gives brief information and facts. Some of the text is just catchy— to grab interest. The second gives more details and focuses on some history and statistics about the space station. The second gives information about life on the space station in much more depth than the first.
4. The first one invites the reader into the action—which fits the purpose of an ad that is trying to get the reader to buy a trip. The highly visual, easy-to-scan structure helps to grab the reader and give quick information about the trip. The second text uses paragraphs to explain details

about the space station and life on the space station. Full sentences are needed to do this.

pages 58–59

Student answers will vary. Look for ideas that are supported by the text. Students might mention that the eyewitness accounts give a different perspective, add information that the detectives had not found, or add believability to the tale.

page 60

1. Lennon's two limousines, Elvis's limousine, and Lennon's recording
2. Answers will vary. The recording sold for about half the cost of the limo. Or, the recording sold for about $90,000 less.
3. Lennon's limousine sold for over two million dollars more.
4. Answers will vary. Information is quick to see and compare.

page 61

1. 8:21 a.m.
2. 10 minutes
3. 5 minutes or less
4. 8 minutes
5. 8:10 a.m.
6. 8:15 a.m.
7. 8:42 a.m.
8. after
9. 8:01 a.m.
10. 5 minutes
11. Answers will vary. Be sure that the explanation makes use of evidence from the text. (Students may choose the third visitor, because he or she was alone in the front room from 8:30 to 8:32 while Ms.

Rathskeller was busy with a phone call.)

page 62

1. Shun Hing Square
2. Petronas Towers
3. Baiyoke II Tower
4. Aon Center and T & C Tower
5. Empire State Building
6. Jin Mao Building
7. John Hancock Center
8. Empire State Building
9. Baiyoke II Tower
10. Petronas Towers

page 63

1. no
2. Zurich, Basel, or Bern
3. Drop 2 or Drop 3
4. no
5. Tuesday, Friday
6. no
7. Drop 2
8. yes
9. 2
10. 4

pages 64–65

Answers on all questions will vary some.

1. Opening paragraph states this. Second paragraph lists some.
2. The whole article seems to invite the public as it describes the wonders of the event. Third paragraph, "food and fun for everyone;" fourth paragraph says so outright.
3. Outside slugs are drug tested. The article says that many slugs are found in the park by the park rangers. It is assumed these are for sure drug free. But because the race is competitive,

officials want to be sure that outside slugs have not been given drugs to give them an unfair speed advantage.
4. He tells about the drug tests. He says park rangers already are looking for speedy slugs.
5. long one—by the number of trophies given and the phrase "several categories"

page 66

Answers will vary.

1. He fights fiercely. He steps right up to the dragon—in spite of the dragon's dangers. He plunges his lance into the dragon.
2. Descriptions show dragon as menacing, fire-breathing, with powerful tail and terrible claws. The writer tells that the dragon has terrorized villages and threatened the castle.
3. There is no evidence of this in the text other than the claim that she is grateful. Actually, the prince did not rescue her at all. The damsel looks to be smitten with the horse.

pages 67–68

Student notes will vary. Check to see that notes are informed by details from the two texts and possibly the illustration.

Reading: Foundational Skills (pages 70–78)

page 70

Answers may vary some.

1. one form
2. on shore
3. make little

4. below standard
5. read wrong
6. state too much
7. middle of the stream
8. against crime
9. across the ocean
10. on foot
11. visit again
12. before the season
13. with many talents
14. not movable
15. small skirt
16. among nations
17. not spoiled
18. not pleased

page 71

horrify–cause horror
amazement–quality of being amazed
wavy–full of waves
strengthen–make strong
dreadful–full of dread
rudderless–without a rudder
wooden–made of wood
backward–toward the back
heroic–like a hero
scientific–pertaining to science
endless–without end
courageous–full of courage
survivor–one who survives
liquefy–to make liquid
dangerous–full of danger
droplets–small drops
troublesome–full of trouble
gladness–state of being glad
sailor–one who sails
heroism–quality of a hero

page 72

1. thermometer
2. geology
3. cooperate
4. projectile
5. captain
6. fraction
7. review
8. immobile
9. ignition

10. autograph
11. gyration
12. donation
13. aquatic
14. fracture
15. actor
16. dynamic

page 73

Answers will vary. Check to see that words are real and use a root and one or more affixes.

page 74

Answers will vary. Check to see that words are real compound words.

page 75

1. break, pier
2. build, pier
3. buried
4. surf
5. lone, beach
6. wave
7. cache
8. feat
9. current
10. cruise
11. crews, sculls
12. oar
13. taut
14. dense

page 76

1. wade, weighed
2. wear, where
3. rode, rowed
4. hear, here
5. eye, Aye, aye
6. pause, paws
7. toad, towed
8. whether, weather
9. wail, whale
10. seen, scene

page 77

1. b   6. b   11. a
2. a   7. b   12. a
3. a   8. c   13. b
4. c   9. c
5. b   10. a

page 78

1. c   6. a   11. a
2. c   7. c   12. b
3. a   8. a   13. c
4. b   9. c
5. b   10. b

Writing (pages 80–96)

pages 80–81

Check to see that letter has a beginning, clearly stated opinion and reasons, and a clear ending.

page 82

Check to see that written paragraphs have clearly stated argument.

page 83

Check to see that text has clear beginning, middle, and end, and that it gives information clearly and sequentially.

page 84

Check to see that writing includes sensible ingredients and equipment (all that are needed) and clear instructions in logical sequence.

page 85

Check to see that story has a clear beginning, plot, and ending and includes exaggeration.

pages 86–87

Check to see that story has a clear beginning, plot, and ending and includes correctly written dialogue. Check to see that illustration relates to the story.

page 88

Check to see that the event is developed, and that the piece has a satisfying beginning and ending.

page 89

Check to see that writing follows the pattern and instructions for painted poems.

page 90–91

Check for logical questions relating to the topics.

pages 92–93

Look for a collection of relevant words for each character, including fitting character names.

Check for descriptive words, "facts," and central and supporting ideas one would gain from a pretend interview.

page 94

1. Look for an original image of the tightrope walk across the Grand Canyon.
2. Look for a well-organized article that matches the visual idea.

page 95

Check for a clear, logical description of a character, event, or setting. Look for references to specific details from the story.

page 96

Check for statement of a main point and a logical, coherent description of evidence.

Language (pages 98–126)

page 98

1. because
2. before
3. even though
4. unless
5. Not only . . . but also
6. Neither . . . nor
7. as . . . as
8. whether . . . or

page 99

1. below the deck; below; deck
2. instead of dinner; instead; dinner
3. below deck Four; below; Deck Four
4. without my permission; without; permission

5–8. Answers will vary. Check to see that student has inserted some correct prepositions and objects.

page 100

1. Stop!
2. Oh! No!
3. Good luck!
4. Whew!
5. Shh!
6. Absolutely!

7–11. Answers will vary. Check to see that student has inserted some correct interjections

page 101

1. yes
2. yes
3. no
4. yes

5–7. Answers will vary. Check to see that perfect tense is used.

page 102

Answers may vary some. Check to see that they fit the verb description.

a. have been harnessing
b. is coming; call; or am wrestling
c. is coming; call; or am wrestling
d. caught; was eating; devoured; or got
e. caught; was eating; devoured; or got
f. caught; was eating; devoured; or got
g. caught; was eating; devoured; or got
h. will soon find; will keep filling; or shall never tell
i. will keep filling
j. got

page 103

Fixes may differ.

1. *Avoid* and *should swim* are different tenses. Change *should swim* to *swim.*
2. *Can get* and *is* are different tenses. Change *is* to *will be.*
3. *Won't be swimming* and *are* are different tenses. Change *are not* to *will not be.*
4. *Can swim* and

wasn't are different tenses. Change *wasn't* to *isn't.*

5. *See* and *Was hiding* are different tenses. Change *Was* to *Is.*

page 104

1. to separate the *No* from the rest of the sentence
2. to separate the question *isn't it?* from the rest of the sentence
3. to separate the introductory phrase *Until this incident* from the rest of the sentence
4. to separate the address to a person from the rest of the sentence
5. to separate items in a series
6. after *Normally*
7. after *edge*
8. after *sunset*
9. after *Lexie, Jamal,* and *Todd*
10. after *Hey*
11. after *Abby*
12. after *toe*

page 105

1. yes
2. yes
3. no—place commas after *Twister* and *Corkscrew*
4. no comma after *House*; insert comma after *Jonas*
5. no—place comma after *Hey*
6. no—place comma after *racetrack*
7. yes
8. no—place comma after *dog*
9. no—delete comma after *dog*; insert comma after *Yes*
10. yes

page 106

1. Rap Singer Meets Sea Urchin
2. "Ode to the Seashore"

3. The Lady and the Octopus
4. Deep Sea Mystery
5. "How to Act Like a Star"
6. Girl with the Golden Surfboard
7. "I'm Just a Hoarse Little Seahorse"
8. Underwater Melodies
9. Secrets of the Starfish
10. "How to be Glamorous Under Water"

page 107

1. absence, breathe, different
2. forty, grief
3. jealous, laundry
4. opposite, recognize
5. terrific, vegetable
6. lovely, twelfth
7. separate
8. people, surprise
9. elephant, mosquito
10. cocoa, every, among
11. paid, toward
12. magnify, excuse

page 108

1. achieve
2. neither
3. biscuit
4. occasionally
5. license
6. restaurant
7. library
8. performance
9. dollar
10. laser
11. chocolate
12. tongue
13. exercise
14. journey
15. pajamas

page 109

The misspelled words (spelled correctly) are: excuse, using, biting, fourth, enough, lovely, breeze, definitely, paradise, complete, picnic, troubles

page 110

Answers will vary. Check to see that

student responses show successful adaptations of sentences to fulfill the directions.

page 111

Answers will vary. Check to see that student responses show successful adaptations of sentences to fulfill the directions.

page 112

Substitutions for statements will vary. Check to see that student adequately understands and can represent the difference between formal and informal use of English.

1. informal
2. formal
3. informal
4. formal
5. informal
6. formal
7. formal
8. formal
9. informal
10. informal

page 113

Guesses will vary. Check to see that they are close to the definition—or a reasonable definition, based on the sentence.
Definitions:

1. perked up, picked up, refreshed
2. muddy, murky
3. changeable
4. dangerous
5. standing still
6. gloomy
7. quick to change
8. unbelievable
9. rude, coarse
10. tiny

page 114

1. intended
2. washed; huge
3. cliff
4. tornado
5. tossed; storm
6. dragged; hid
7. ocean; earthquake
8. shook; ship
9. crashed; sank
10. mystery

page 115

1. minority
2. diagnosis
3. simmer
4. annuals
5. principal
6. copyright
7. circumference
8. hurricane
9. translucent
10. accept

page 116

Check drawings for accuracy and to see that student understands the word meanings.

page 117

1. treacherous
2. diver
3. magical
4. deepen
5. frighten
Answer: a tiger shark
6. skyward
7. hungry
8. oceanic
9. breakable
10. sharpness
Answer: a whale shark

page 118

Answers may vary. Discuss these. Accept any reasonable explanations.

1. yes   9. no
2. no   10. yes
3. no   11. yes
4. no   12. no
5. yes   13. no
   or   14. yes/
   no   no
6. no   (personal
7. yes   preference)
8. no   15. no

page 119

Answers may vary. Discuss these. Accept any reasonable explanations.

1. fry it for lunch
2. feed it to fish
3. take it swimming
4. put it in a jewelry box
5. avoid it
6. explore it
7. find an answer to it
8. dance it
9. bake it
10. show it off
11. hold on to it
12. make music on it
13. make friends with it
14. send it to school
15. pour water through it
16. hire it

page 120

The number of examples students find may vary, depending upon how they interpret whether something is a metaphor. cost me an arm and a leg; sun beating on me; seagulls squawking as loud as a rock band; chip off the old block; pretty as a picture; faster than greased lightning; dry as dust; as dull as a doorknob; red-letter day; go bananas; blow her top; go off her rocker; take the cake; breaking up ships like toothpicks; scared stiff; screaming bloody murder; the last straw; out of sight, out of mind; absence makes the heart grow fonder; snap my fingers and you'd be here; quick as a wink; make no bones about it; today is a wipe-out; deader than a doornail

page 121

Explanations may vary some. Drawings should show literal meaning.

Go out on a limb.—
Take a risk.

You've spilled the beans.—
You've told some information or secrets.

It's raining cats and dogs.—
It's raining very hard.

I have a bone to pick with you.—
I have an issue with you.

You drive me up a wall.—
You are bothering me—seriously!

My car's a real lemon.—
My car has all kinds of things wrong with it.

She's lost her head!—
She is not thinking clearly.

Don't jump the gun.—
Don't do something too soon.

page 122

What a backseat driver!—
This passenger tells the driver how to drive.

This will cook your goose.—
This will upset you.

Jay likes to ham it up.—
Jay likes to be funny.

It's the last straw!—
It is one of many problems—the last one that makes me feel that I have had enough.

Keep a lid on it!—
Be quiet. Or, don't tell.

Don't lose your cool.—
Stay calm.

She's got her nose in a book.—
She is reading a book and has blocked out everything else.

You've put your foot in your mouth again.—
You have said something embarrassing or inappropriate.

page 123

Path from top crab to bottom crab:
rubbish, garbage—
infant, newborn—
bandit, robber—
applaud, clap—
dull, dreary—
precise, exact—
triumph, victory—
essential, necessary

page 124

Answers will vary. Check to see that words are replaced with antonyms
Here are possibilities:
Replace *dream* with *nightmare.*
Replace *sunrise* with *sunset.*
Replace *terrible* with *delicious.*
Replace *valuables* with *trash.*
Replace *waking* with *sleeping.*
Replace *shallow* with *deep.*
Replace *closed* with *open.*
Replace *straight* with *crooked.*
Replace *smallest* with *largest.*
Replace *returns* with *steals.*
Replace *midnight* with *noon.*

page 125

Answer to top question: wail

1. see; sea
2. son, sun
3. heard, herd
4. steal, steel
5. Would, wood
6. groan, grown
7. weak, week
8. not, knot
9. ate, eight
10. close, clothes
11. toe, tow
12. sore, soar

page 126

Down

1. abalone
2. ecology
3. habitat
4. grotto
7. tsunami
8. mariner
10. weed

Across

5. trough
6. ichthyologist
9. flotsam
11. archipelago
12. fjord
13. sea